Foundations of Modern Sociology Series
Alex Inkeles, *Editor*

The Sociology of Ideology, *Daniel Bell*
Science and Society, *Joseph Ben-David*
Deviance and Control, *Albert K. Cohen*
Modern Organizations, *Amitai Etzioni*
The Family, *William J. Goode*
Society and Population, *David Heer*
What Is Sociology? An Introduction to the Discipline and Profession, *Alex Inkeles*
Theory and Method in the Social Sciences, *Paul F. Lazarsfeld*
Person and Society: An Introduction to Social Psychology,
Daniel J. Levinson and Alex Inkeles
The Sociology of Small Groups, *Theodore M. Mills*
Social Change, *Wilbert E. Moore*
The Sociology of Religion, *Thomas F. O'Dea*
Societies: Evolutionary and Comparative Perspectives, *Talcott Parsons*
The System of Modern Societies, *Talcott Parsons*
Community Social Structure, *Peter H. Rossi*
Changing Rural Societies, *Irwin T. Sanders*
The American School: A Sociological Analysis, *Patricia C. Sexton*
The Sociology of Economic Life, *Neil J. Smelser*
Social Stratification: The Forms and Functions of Inequality, *Melvin M. Tumin*

Foundations of Modern Sociology Series

societies

EVOLUTIONARY AND COMPARATIVE PERSPECTIVES

Talcott Parsons, *Harvard University*

Prentice-Hall, Inc., *Englewood Cliffs, New Jersey*

Prentice-Hall Foundations of Modern Sociology Series

Alex Inkeles, *Editor*

Printed in the United States of America.
Library of Congress Catalog No.: 65-12343.
Designed by Harry Rinehart

Current printing (last digit):
11 10 9 8 7 6 5 4 3

PRENTICE-HALL INTERNATIONAL, INC., *London*
PRENTICE-HALL OF AUSTRALIA, PTY., LTD., *Sydney*
PRENTICE-HALL OF CANADA, LTD., *Toronto*
PRENTICE-HALL OF INDIA PRIVATE LIMITED, *New Delhi*
PRENTICE-HALL OF JAPAN, INC., *Tokyo*

C—81962(p), C—81963(c)

preface

When the editor of the *Foundations of Modern Sociology Series,* Alex Inkeles, asked the author to contribute a volume dealing with the total society as a social system, it was a tempting assignment, but one that also has turned out to be unexpectedly difficult. It went without saying that the perspective of the book should be comparative, that the theoretical resources of sociology should be mobilized to analyze not only the interconnections of different parts of the same society and the forces operating to change its structure, but also the variations of type as between different societies.

The comparative emphasis, however, confronted one directly with the problem of dealing with societal evolution, and this was accepted as an obligation that could not properly be evaded—all the more so because the recent increase in the concern of social scientists with comparative problems and the resultant volume of research contributions have posed the problems of evolution with a renewed definiteness and urgency. This has also been stimulated by new developments in the unification of scientific theory, particularly in this case between the biological and the social sciences.

These decisions generated severe problems concerning the selection of empirical materials and their theoretical ordering and analysis. Obviously, to do anything like full "justice" to such problems would require a very extended treatise, probably of several volumes. The severe space limitations of volumes in the present series precluded anything like this. Even so, the first full draft far exceeded the limit; the editor and the publisher kindly agreed to permit the material with the appropriate reorganization to be divided between two volumes in the series. The division between them has been made in terms of evolutionary stage. Hence the present volume will stop with a survey of the principal societies which are classified as "advanced intermediate," including the two dealt with in Chapter 6 as "Seed-bed" societies, namely ancient Israel and classical Greece. The present volume then will be followed by the *System of Modern Societies,* dealing with the system which originated only in one time and place, Europe after the Middle Ages, though of course its basic structural patterns have now spread outside Europe. The two volumes are designed to be sufficiently independent so that each can be read without depending on the other. The author's more general thinking on the problem of comparative and evolutionary analysis of societies, however, can best be understood by taking the two together.

Any enterprise such as this, especially when it extends over a considerable period, inevitably involves critically important contributions from many besides the author himself. Alex Inkeles, as editor of the series, has been uniformly understanding and helpful, as have been the personnel of Prentice-Hall, Inc., with whom I have dealt. Another important debt of gratitude is owed to Miss Constance Barron, who as my secretary has been primarily responsible for processing the manuscript. A particularly heavy obligation, however, is owed to Victor M. Lidz, whose services have been completely indispensable. As my research assistant, he has been the principal seeker and winnower of literature. In long discussions of the empirical and interpretive problems, he has contributed enormously to clarification and systematization of the analysis. Finally, he has edited all the manuscript material in the interest of clarity and style. Without his help nothing closely resembling the present book could have been written.

Talcott Parsons

contents

the study of societies, 1
one

the concept of society:
the components and their interrelations, 5
two

The General Conceptual Scheme of Action. The Concept of Social System. The Concept of Society. The Societal Community and Its Environments. The Societal Community and Self-sufficiency. The Structural Components of Societies. Process and Change. A Paradigm of Evolutionary Change. The Differentiation of the Subsystems of Society. Stages in the Evolution of Societies.

three **primitive societies, 30**

The Components of Primitive Society.
The Primitive Society of Aboriginal Australia.
The Transition to the "Advanced" Primitive Type.
Types of Advanced Primitive Societies.

four **archaic societies, 51**

Ancient Egypt.
The Mesopotamian Empires.

five **the "historic" intermediate empires, 69**

China. India.
The Islamic Empires.
The Roman Empire. Conclusion.

six **two "seed-bed" societies: Israel and Greece, 95**

Israel. Greece.

seven **conclusion, 109**

selected references, 116

index, 118

the study of societies

one

The series of books called the Foundations of Modern Sociology, of which this small book is a part, deals with societies and their constituent parts from a number of viewpoints and at a number of levels. Some volumes deal mainly with small constituent elements such as the family or the local community, others with special topics such as theory and method of study. This book stands at one extreme in that it treats the most comprehensive unit ordinarily studied by sociologists, the *total society*. There is, to be sure, an immense variety of types of societies, ranging all the way from extremely small-scale primitive societies to the new supernational societies of the United States and the Soviet Union. Furthermore, at approximately equivalent levels of development, there are also wide ranges of variation, such as from the ascriptive rigidities of the traditional Indian caste system to the relative openness and mobility of the Chinese Empire. In this essay we will try to bring some order to this very complex subject.

Treating societies as wholes by no means exhausts the possibilities for empirical application of the concept of the social system. Many social systems such as local communities, schools, business firms, and kinship units are not societies, but rather sub-systems of a society. Also, in a sufficiently pluralistic world, many social systems, which are "partial" systems in terms of the concept of society, may be parts of more than one society. The simplest cases involve interpenetrating membership. Thus, the emigration of a nuclear family makes it, by stages, a structural unit in the society to which it moves. Many relatives, however, remain in the "old country." Together with the migrating family, they certainly constitute social systems which penetrate or overlap two or more societies. The same can be said of business firms, professional associations, churches, and other organizations which maintain "branches" in two or more countries. There is, finally, a sense in which a society is not the most extensive social system, but is part of a still broader international or intersocietal system.

The concept of society will be more fully discussed in the next chapter. For the moment, it suffices to say that a society is relatively the most self-sufficient type of social system. A society internally integrates more of the requisites of independent existence than do units like a business firm, which is too specialized, or "Christendom," which is too loosely organized to function in concert as a single society. Therefore, insofar as they are differentiated or segmented, units of a society are more dependent on other units of the same society than on units of other societies.

For reasons discussed below, a society is in the first instance "politically organized," to use Roscoe Pound's phrase. It must have loyalties both to a sense of community and to some "corporate agency" of the kind we ordinarily consider governmental, and must establish a relatively effective normative order within a territorial area.

In our study of societies we will be guided by both an evolutionary and a comparative perspective. The former conceives of man as integral to the organic world, and human society and culture as properly analyzed in the general framework appropriate to the life process. Whether the adjective "biological" be used or not, the principle of evolution is firmly established as applying to the world of living things. Here the social aspect of human life must be included. Such basic concepts of organic evolution as variation, selection, adaptation, differentiation, and integration belong at the center of our concern, when appropriately adjusted to social and cultural subject matter.

Socio-cultural evolution, like organic evolution, has proceeded by variation and differentiation from simple to progressively more complex forms. Contrary to some early conceptions in the field, however, it has not proceeded in a single neatly definable line, but at every level has included a rather wide variety of different forms and types.[1] Nevertheless, longer perspectives make it evident that forms apparently equally viable in given stages and circumstances have not been equal in terms of their potentialities for contributing to further evolutionary developments. Still, the immense variability of human patterns of action is one of the most important facts about the human condition.

Seen in this light, there are four interdependent yet in certain respects independent aspects of the theoretical problems facing us. First, we must use the general conceptual scheme of the social system which underlies all sociological analysis, whatever the size and functional importance of the system of reference relative to other systems.

Second, we must consider the problems of the society that arise from its being a type of social system which is more inclusive of controls over action than all others and which hence has special features requiring special analysis. The study of societies, which is our subject matter, is not identical with the study of social systems generally.[2]

[1] In biological theory, variation is conceived as a crucial factor in evolution operating at every level of development. In overlooking its fundamental importance, the early social evolutionists fell far short of developing a truly evolutionary perspective.

[2] Cf. Talcott Parsons, "Social Systems and Subsystems," in the forthcoming *International Encyclopedia of the Social Sciences*.

Third, we must be concerned with the evolutionary development of societies, both as wholes and in their principal structural parts. We are concerned with the sequences of changing structural patterns which characterize societies as social systems in the course of their evolution and, as far as limitations both of knowledge and of space permit, with the processes by which the transitions have occurred. We hope to delineate certain fairly coherent patterns of order in these respects.

Finally, we must also consider variability as a problem distinct from—but interdependent with—that of evolutionary stage and sequence. The mere fact that the cultural, physical, biological, psychological, and social environments of societies, as of other social systems, are highly variable is reason enough to expect that the societies, being interdependent with these environmental factors as well as autonomous, will also vary considerably. Some attempts to specify the variations found at different stages of evolution, the reasons for them, and the potentialities for their further development are essential to an investigation such as this.

The next chapter will present a very broad—and tentative—schema that divides the evolution of societies (so far) into three stages: primitive, intermediate, and modern. The substantive analysis of this book will treat only the first two categories. Moreover, its bulk will be devoted to intermediate societies, partly because they show a wider and more significant range of variation than primitive societies and partly because our neighboring discipline, social anthropology, has studied primitive societies so extensively and intensively. There are many anthropological studies that approach primitive societies in comparative and evolutionary terms. But intermediate societies have been studied mainly by archaeologists, historians, linguists, and other specialists who are oriented more to particular civilizations or to particular aspects of socio-cultural structure than to very general comparisons.

The present author is preparing a sequel to this volume that will appear in the Foundations of Modern Sociology Series under the title *The System of Modern Societies*. The two books are designed to be read separately, but they are both conceived, very largely, in relation to one broad empirical problem. Thus it will help those who may read both volumes to make certain features of that problem explicit here. Also, it will clarify the grounds for dividing the general consideration of social evolution into two works.

In the author's view, the main organizational patterns of societies of the type justifiably considered modern share a common origin. This origin was comprised of the societies of Western Europe as they developed from the mediaeval base which emerged after the decline of the western Roman Empire. So far, the main structural features of other modern societies are based upon diffusion from this point of origin, though they often involve very important structural innovations (variations) not found in the older West European systems. The most "developed" of such societies are the United States and the Soviet Union, the European origins of which are evident, and Japan, the modernization of which has clearly been a reaction to the impact of the European-American system, however important the influence of indigenous elements may have been.

This thesis, which emphasizes the uniqueness of the original development of the modern societal type in the West, poses certain problems of objectivity for a student who is part of the system he is trying to evaluate. However that may be, our emphasizing the fact of common origin also presents an opportunity —namely, to treat the principal modern societies as constituting a system; i.e., a social system more extensive and differentiated than any one society.

It does not seem that the varieties of primitive and intermediate societies can generally and usefully be regarded as comprising larger systems in the sense of the modern system. This difference provides a natural break between the subject matters of the two books. Furthermore, it provides a challenging set of interpretive problems which will guide our discussion of the more advanced intermediate societies, problems whose significance was classically demonstrated by Max Weber.

The *range* of variation among advanced intermediate societies was very wide—think of the contrasts between the Chinese Empire at its height, the Indian caste system, the Islamic empires, and the Roman Empire! All these societies contained *very* highly developed civilizations. Why, then, did the breakthrough to modernization not occur in *any* of the "Oriental" advanced intermediate civilizations? Conversely, what constellation of factors were involved in its occurrence against the background of the most radical structural regression in the history of major societies—namely, the "fall" of the western Roman Empire and the reversion of its territories to more or less "archaic" social conditions in the "dark ages"? This is the historical-interpretive perspective, as distinct from that of systematic theory, which will guide the analysis of the present book as well as its sequel.

the concept of society: the components and their interrelations

two

As we mentioned, the society is a special kind of social system. We treat the social system as one of the primary subsystems of the human *action* system, the others being the behavioral organism, the personality of the individual, and the cultural system.[1]

The General Conceptual Scheme of Action

Action consists of the structures and processes by which human beings form meaningful intentions and, more or less successfully, implement them in concrete situations. The word "meaningful" implies the symbolic or cultural level of representation and reference. Intentions and implementation taken together imply a disposition of the action system—individual or collective—to modify its relation to its situation or environment in an intended direction.

We prefer the term "action" to "behavior" because we are interested not in the physical events of behavior for their own sake but in their patterning, their patterned meaningful products (physical, cultural, and other), ranging from implements to works of art, and the mechanisms and processes that control such patterning.

Human action is "cultural" in that meanings and intentions concerning acts are formed in terms of *symbolic* systems (including the codes through which they operate in patterns) that focus most generally about the universal of human societies, language.

There is a sense in which all action is the action of individuals. However,

[1] The reader may find it helpful in following this discussion to refer to Tables 1 and 2, appended to this chapter, for graphic representation of the interrelations between these systems.

both the organism and the cultural system involve essential elements which cannot be investigated at the individual level.

For the organism, the primary structural reference is not the anatomy of the particular organism, but the *species-type*.[2] To be sure, this type does not actualize itself, but works through the genetic constitutions of unique individual organisms, which involve both varying combinations of the genetic materials characteristic of the species and the effects of different environmental conditions. But however important individual variations may be in determining concrete action, it is the common patterns of large human groups—including their differentiation into two sexes—which constitute the massive organic sub-stratum of action.

It would not be correct to say that the genetic constitution of an organism is modified by environmental influence. Rather, the genetic constitution comprises a general "orientation" which develops into specific anatomical structures, physiological mechanisms, and behavioral patternings as it interacts with environmental factors during the life of the organism. The environmental factors can be analyzed into two categories: first, those responsible for the non-hereditary elements of the physical organism; second, those responsible for the *learned* elements of behavioral systems, which is the category upon which we must focus. Although an organism may certainly be capable of learning in immediate environments devoid of other behaving organisms, the theory of action is primarily concerned with learning in which other organisms of the same species constitute the most important feature of the general environment.

Symbolically *organized* cultural patterns, like all other components of living systems, have certainly emerged through evolution. Yet, the human linguistic *level* of their development is a phenomenon entirely unique to man. The capacity to learn and use language clearly depends on man's special genetic constitution, as the failure of attempts to teach it to other species (especially the primates and "talking" birds) has shown.[3] But only this general capacity is genetically determined, *not* the specific symbolic systems which are actually learned, used, and developed by specific human groups.

Furthermore, despite the great capacity of human organisms for learning and, indeed, for creating cultural elements, no individual can create a cultural system. The *main* patternings of cultural systems change only over periods of many generations and are *always* shared by relatively large groups; they are never special to one or a few individuals. Therefore, they are always learned by the individual, who can make only rather marginal creative (or destructive) contributions to their change. Thus the more general cultural patterns provide action systems with a highly stable structural anchorage quite analogous to that provided by the genetic materials of the species-type, focusing on the learned elements of action just as the genes focus upon the inheritable elements.[4]

[2] Good modern reviews of evolutionary biology are *The Meaning of Evolution* by George Gaylord Simpson (New Haven: Yale University Press, 1950); and *Animal Species and Evolution* by Ernst Mayr (Cambridge: Harvard University Press, 1963).

[3] See Chap. V in *Words and Things* by Roger Brown (Glencoe, Ill.: The Free Press, 1958).

[4] This point has been clearly stated by Alfred Emerson in "Homeostasis and Comparison of Systems" in Roy Grinker (ed.), *Toward a Unified Theory of Human Behavior* (New York: Basic Books, 1956), pp. 147–162, especially p. 152.

Within the limits imposed by the genetic species-type on the one hand, and the patterning of the culture on the other, lies the opportunity for given individuals and groups to develop independently structured behavioral systems. Because an actor is genetically human, and because his learning occurs in the context of a particular cultural system, his learned behavioral system (which I shall call his personality) shares certain broad features with other personalities—e.g., the language he habitually speaks. At the same time, his organism and its environment—physical, social, and cultural—are always in certain respects unique. Hence, his own behavioral system will be a *unique variant* of the culture and its particular patterns of action. It is therefore essential to consider the personality system as not reducible to either the organism or the culture—*what* is learned is part of neither the "structure" of the organism in the usual sense nor a feature of the cultural system. It comprises an *analytically independent system.*[5]

Though intimately intertwined with the personalities of the interacting individuals and the patterns of the cultural system, the process of social interaction forms a fourth system that is analytically independent of both personal and cultural systems, as well as of the organism.[6] This independence becomes most evident in regard to the requirements for integration that impinge upon systems of social relationships because of their inherent potential for conflict and disorganization. This is sometimes known as the *problem of order* in society, posed in classic form by Thomas Hobbes.[7] The system of interaction constitutes the social system, the sub-system of action with which this book is primarily concerned.

The above classification of four highly general sub-systems of human action—the organism, personality, social system, and cultural system—is an application of a general paradigm which can be used throughout the field of action, and which I shall use below to analyze social systems. This paradigm analyzes *any* action *system* in terms of the following four functional categories: (1) that concerned with the maintenance of the highest "governing" or controlling patterns of the system; (2) the internal integration of the system; (3) its orientation to the attainment of goals in relation to its environment; (4) its more generalized adaptation to the broad conditions of the environment—e.g., the non-action, physical environment. Within action systems, cultural systems are specialized around the function of pattern-maintenance, social systems around the integration of acting units (human individuals or, more precisely, personalities engaged in roles), personality systems around goal-attainment, and the behavioral organism around adaptation (see Table 1).

[5] A more detailed discussion of the relations of the personality to the other sub-systems of action is contained in Jesse R. Pitts, "Introduction" to Part Three of *Theories of Society;* Talcott Parsons, Edward A. Shils, Kasper D. Naegele, and Jesse R. Pitts (eds.) (New York: The Free Press of Glencoe, 1961).

[6] "Some Fundamental Categories of the Theory of Action," the general collaborative essay, and "Values, Motives and Systems of Action," the contribution of Talcott Parsons and Edward A. Shils in *Toward a General Theory of Action* (Cambridge: Harvard University Press, 1951). Also see Talcott Parsons, "Interaction," in the forthcoming *International Encyclopedia of the Social Sciences.*

[7] I used Hobbes' statement as a major point of departure for my own treatment of the theory of the social system in *Structure of Social Action* (New York: McGraw-Hill, 1937).

The Concept of the Social System

Since the social system is made up of the interaction of human individuals, each member is *both actor* (having goals, ideas, attitudes, etc.) *and object* of orientation for *both* other actors and himself. The interaction system, then, is an *analytical aspect abstractable* from the total action processes of its participants. At the same time, these "individuals" are also organisms, personalities, and participants in cultural systems.

Because of such interpenetration, each of the other three action systems (Culture, Personality, Behavioral Organism) constitutes a part of the environment—or, we may say *an* environment—of a social system. Beyond these systems are the environments of action itself, standing above and below the general hierarchy of factors that control action in the world of life. These relationships are depicted in Table 1.

Below action in the hierarchy stands the physical-organic environment, including the sub-human species of organisms and the "nonbehavioral" components of human organisms. This is a particularly important boundary of action because, as humans, we know the physical world *only* through the organism. Our minds have no direct experience of an external physical object unless we perceive it through physical processes and the brain "processes" information about it. In their psychologically known sense, however, physical objects are aspects of action.

In principle, similar considerations apply to the environment above action—the "ultimate reality" with which we are ultimately concerned in grappling with what Weber called the "problems of meaning"—e.g., evil and suffering, the temporal limitations of human life, and the like. "Ideas" in this area, as cultural objects, are in some sense symbolic "representations" (e.g., conceptions of gods, totems, the supernatural) of the ultimate realities, but are not themselves such realities.

A fundamental principle about the organization of living systems is that their structures are differentiated in regard to the various exigencies imposed upon them by their environments. Thus the biological functions of respiration, nutrition-elimination, locomotion, and information-processing are bases of differentiated organ-systems, each of which is specialized about the exigencies of certain relations between the organism and its environment. We will use this principle to organize our analysis of social systems.

We will consider social systems in their relations to their most important environments. I will contend that the functional differentiations among the three sub-systems of action other than the social—the cultural system, the personality system, and the behavioral organism—and the articulation of two of them with the two environments of the entire action system, constitute very major references for analyzing the differences among social systems. That is, my analysis will be developed on the basis of the fundamental system-and-environment relations of Table 1.

In the functional terms of our paradigm, the social system is the *integrative* sub-system of action in general. The other three sub-systems of action constitute principal environments in relation to it. In the analysis of societies or other social systems, then, the above principle can be applied. We will see that three of the primary sub-systems of the society (Table 2, column III) are functionally specialized around their interrelations with the three principal environments of a social system (Table 2, column IV), each relating most directly to one of these environments. Each of these three societal sub-systems may also be considered a distinct environment of the sub-system which is the society's integrative core (Table 2, column II). We will employ this *dual* application of the functional paradigm throughout the exposition of our general theoretical scheme, and in the analysis of particular societies in the body of the book.[8]

The Concept of Society

In defining a society, we may use a criterion which goes back at least to Aristotle. A society is a type of social system, in any universe of social systems, which attains the highest level of self-sufficiency as a system in relation to its environments.

This definition refers to an abstracted system, of which the other, similarly abstracted sub-systems of action are the primary environments. This view contrasts sharply with our common-sense notion of society as being composed of concrete human individuals. Organisms and the personalities of members of the society would then be internal to the society, not part of its environment. We cannot argue the merits of these two views of societies here. But the reader must be clear about the usage in this book.

With this understanding, the criterion of self-sufficiency can be divided into five sub-criteria, each relating to one of the five environments of social systems—Ultimate Reality, Cultural Systems, Personality Systems, Behavioral Organisms, the Physical-Organic Environment. The self-sufficiency of a society is a function of the balanced *combination* of its controls over its relations with these five environments and of its own state of internal integration.

We have referred to a hierarchy of control which organizes the interrelations of the analytically distinguished systems. This includes the *cybernetic* aspect of control by which systems high in information but low in energy regulate other systems higher in energy but lower in information (Table 1, column V).[9] Thus, a programed sequence of mechanical operations (e.g., in a washing machine) can be controlled by a timing switch using very little energy compared with the energy actually operating the machine's moving parts or heating its water. Another example is the gene and its control over protein synthesis and other aspects of cell metabolism.

The cultural system structures commitments vis-à-vis ultimate reality into meaningful orientations toward the rest of the environment and the system of action, the physical world, organisms, personalities, and social systems. In the cybernetic sense, it is highest within the action system, the social system ranking next, and personality and organism falling respectively below that. The

[8] Cf. Talcott Parsons, "Social Systems and Subsystems," in the forthcoming *International Encyclopedia of the Social Sciences*.

[9] The theory of cybernetics was first developed by Norbert Wiener in *Cybernetics* (Cambridge: The M.I.T. Press, 1948, second edition, 1961) and was applied to social problems in his *The Human Use of Human Beings* (Garden City: Anchor Books, 1954). A good introductory statement for the social scientist will be found in Karl W. Deutsch, *The Nerves of Government* (New York: Free Press of Glencoe, 1963).

physical environment is ultimate in the *conditional*, as distinguished from the organizational, sense. Insofar as physical factors are not controllable by the cybernetically higher-order systems, we must adapt to them or human life will disappear. Human dependence on oxygen, food, tolerable temperatures, and so on, are very familiar examples.

Because of our wide evolutionary perspective, our major concern among the non-social sub-systems of action will be with the cultural system. Because they develop over long periods and under widely varying circumstances, forms of social organization emerge which have increasingly broad adaptive capacities. In their broad characteristics, they tend to become decreasingly subject to major change from narrow, particularized, conditional causes operating through specific physical circumstances or individual organic or personality differences. In the more advanced societies, the range of individual personalities may even broaden whereas the structure and processes of the society become less dependent on individual idiosyncracies. Thus we must focus on the cybernetically higher-order structures—the cultural system among the environments of the society—in order to examine the major sources of large-scale change.

The Societal Community and Its Environments [10]

The core of a society, as a system, is the patterned normative order through which the life of a population is collectively organized. As an order, it contains values and differentiated and particularized norms and rules, all of which require cultural references in order to be meaningful and legitimate. As a collectivity, it displays a patterned conception of membership which distinguishes between those individuals who do and do not belong. Problems involving the "jurisdiction" of the normative system may make impossible an exact coincidence between the status of "coming under" normative obligations and the status of membership, because the enforcement of a normative system seems inherently linked to the control (e.g., through the "police function") of sanctions exercised by and against the people actually residing within a territory.[11] Unless these problems become critical, the societal collectivity can act effectively as a unit when required, and so can various of its sub-collectivities.

We will call this one entity of the society, in its collective aspect, the societal community. As such, it is constituted both by a normative system of order *and* by statuses, rights, and obligations pertaining to membership which may vary for different sub-groups within the community. To survive and develop, the social community must maintain the integrity of a common cultural orientation, broadly (though not necessarily uniformly or unanimously) shared by its membership, as the basis of its societal identity. This problem concerns its connection with the superordinate cultural system. However, it must also meet systematically the conditional exigencies regarding the integration of mem-

[10] This section concerns the relations between column II and columns III and IV in Table 2.

[11] Talcott Parsons, "Some Reflections on the Place of Force in Social Process," in Harry Eckstein (ed.), *Internal War: Basic Problems and Approaches* (New York: The Free Press of Glencoe, 1964).

bers' organisms (and their relations to the physical environment) and personalities. All these factors are complexly interdependent, yet each is a focus for the crystallization of a distinctive type of social mechanism.

The Cultural System as Environment to Society [12]

The central functional exigency of the interrelations between a society and a cultural system is the *legitimation* of the society's normative order. Legitimation systems define the reasons for members' rights and for the prohibitions incumbent upon them. Above all, but not exclusively, the use of power requires legitimation. The present concept of legitimation need not imply the adjective "moral" in a modern sense. But it does imply that it is in some sense "right" that things be done in accord with the institutionalized order.

The function of legitimation is independent of the *operative* functions of a social system. No normative order is ever *self*-legitimating in the sense that the approved or prohibited way of life simply *is* right or wrong and admits of no questions. Nor is it ever adequately legitimized by necessities imposed at lower levels of the hierarchy of control—e.g., that things *must* be done in a *specific* way because the stability or even survival of the system is at stake.

However, the *extent* of the culturally-grounded independence between the bases of legitimation and specific lower-order operative mechanisms (e.g., bureaucratic organization and economic markets) is highly variable among societies. By and large, an increase in this independence is a main trend of the evolutonary process, involving differentiation between cultural and societal structures and processes. Whatever its position on this line of development, however, a legitimation system is always related to, and meaningfully dependent on, a grounding in ordered relations to ultimate reality. That is, its grounding is always in some sense religious. In quite primitive societies, there actually is little differentiation between the general structures of a society and its religious organization. In more advanced societies, the interrelation of social and cultural systems in the religious and legitimation contexts involves highly specialized and complicated structures.

Cultural value patterns provide the most direct link between the social and cultural systems in legitimizing the normative order of the society. The mode of legitimation in turn is grounded in religious orientations. As cultural systems become more differentiated, however, other cultural structures assume increasing independent importance, particularly the arts, which have special relations to the autonomy of personalities and empirical cognitive knowledge, which at an advanced level becomes science.

Personality as Environment to Society

A society's relation to the personality system differs radically from its relation to the cultural system, because the personality (like the behavioral organism and the physical-organic environment) stands *below* the social system in the cybernetic hierarchy. The society as a system, and *each*

[12] The following three sections concern relations obtaining between columns III and IV in Table 2.

of its constituent units, is subject to constraining conditions—which are also opportunities to be utilized—in each of these three contexts. Behavior, of which social systems comprise one analytical aspect, is always in another aspect the behavior *of* living human organisms. Every such organism has at any given moment a given location in physical space which can be changed only through physical motion. Hence, the ecological aspect of the relations among individuals and their actions is never safely neglected. Similar considerations apply to organic processes and to personality functioning and development, both of which are also constantly present as factors of concrete action. Exigencies relating to personalities, behavioral organisms, and the physical-organic environment account for many of the complex, cross-cutting dimensions of the actual organization and functioning of social systems, which require careful analysis and which constantly raise difficulties for social scientists.

The major functional problem concerning the social system's relation to the personality system involves learning, developing, and maintaining through the life cycle adequate motivation for participating in socially valued and controlled patterns of action. Reciprocally, a society must also adequately satisfy or reward its members through such patterns of action, if it is continually to draw upon their performances for its functioning as a system. This relationship constitutes "socialization," the whole complex of processes by which persons become members of the societal community and maintain that status.

Since personality is the *learned organization* of the behaving individual, the socialization process is always critical to its formation and functioning. Successful socialization requires that social and cultural learning be strongly motivated through the engagement of the pleasure mechanisms of the organism. Hence, it depends on relatively stable intimate relations between young children and adults, whose own erotic motives and relations tend to be deeply engaged too. This complex of exigencies, which we have come to understand much more fully since Freud, is an essential aspect of the functioning of kinship systems in all human societies. Kinship always involves an ordering of the erotic relations of adults, of their statuses in relation to presumptive parenthood, of the statuses of the new generation, and of the socialization process itself.[13] It is an evolutionary universal found in *all* societies, though its forms and relations to other structural complexes vary enormously.

A kinship system requires some stable arrangements for day-to-day living which involve organic and psychological as well as social factors. Hence it is a zone of interpenetration among behavioral, personality, and social systems and the physical environment. The latter reference involves the institutionalization of *residence* with respect to location and the constitution of the social unit we call the *household*. The household members are the people who live together as a unit. They share a definite location with physical arrangements, such as a hut or house, or in temporary settlements, a "camp." In most societies, people normally sleep, prepare and eat most of their food, and carry on at least most formally approved sexual activity in that physical and social setting. The household unit is, with all its variations, perhaps the primordial unit of solidarity in social systems.

Although its forms vary greatly, adult status involves the assumption of

[13] Cf. Talcott Parsons and Robert F. Bales, *Family, Socialization, and Interaction Process* (Glencoe, Ill.: The Free Press, 1955).

a certain amount of autonomous responsibility in all societies. The individual performs *services* in some context of collective organization. As a product of a long evolutionary process, these performances become institutionalized in modern societies primarily around the occupational role in a specific-function collectivity, or bureaucratic organization. In any case, the *primary* functional relation between adult individuals and their societies concerns the contributions adults make through performing services and the satisfactions or rewards they derive from them. In sufficiently differentiated societies, capacity for service becomes a mobile resource of the society, mobilizable through the market. When this stage is reached, we can speak of services as an output of the economic process, available for "consumption" in non-economic connections.

For most people in most societies, the places of residence and work are not differentiated. Where this differentiation does occur (mainly in advanced urban communities), these *two* locations constitute the locational axis of the individual's more routine life. Furthermore, the two places must be mutually accessible, a functional requirement about which the major ecological structure of modern cities is generally formed.

A variety of functional relations between personalities and their environments must be treated in other contexts relative to the social system. An individual's value-commitments and their maintenance link primarily with the cultural system, especially as it interrelates with the society through religion. The maintenance of adequate levels of motivation involves mainly the social structures concerned with socialization, particularly kinship. Although physical health is another matter, it shades complexly into the important but vague areas of mental health and the will of the sick to regain health. It seems that *no* society is without motivation-maintenance mechanisms that operate through some kind of "therapeutic" procedures.[14] In many societies these procedures are predominantly religious or magical, but in modern societies they have been emerging into an applied science. Yet, in no case are they radically dissociated from kinship on a society-wide basis—rather, therapy generally supplements kinship, which is the focal support for the security of personalities.

Surprising as it may seem, the relation between personality and social system, socially structured through what we have called *service*, provides the basic unit for the *political* aspect of societies.[15] Political structures are concerned with organizing collective action for the attainment of collectively significant goals, whether on a society-wide basis or on more narrow bases, either territorially or functionally defined. Advanced political development requires status-differentiation within the adult population on some combination of two bases. The first involves levels of responsibility for coordinated collective action and grounds the institutions of leadership and authority. The second concerns levels of competence, based on knowledge, skill, and the like, and assigns greater influence in collective deliberations to the more competent. A political system's differentiation from the matrix of the societal community involves institutionalizing higher-order statuses in both these contexts, often in

[14] Cf. Benjamin Nelson, "Self-Images and Systems of Spiritual Direction in the History of European Civilization," in S. Z. Klausner (ed.), *The Quest for Self-Control* (New York: The Free Press of Glencoe, 1965).

[15] Talcott Parsons, "The Political Aspect of Social Structure and Process," in David Easton (ed.), *Varieties of Political Theory* (Englewood Cliffs, N.J.: Prentice-Hall, 1966).

very complex combinations. The relation of such statuses to religious leadership, particularly the degree of differentiation between leadership in religious and in political contexts, may also present major complications. The imperative of legitimation, not only of the societal order, but also of political authority in particular, indicates a main context of such complications.

Lower in the cybernetic hierarchy is another basis of complication. As we mentioned earlier, the maintenance of a normative order requires that it be implemented in a variety of respects; there must be very considerable—even if often quite incomplete—compliance with the behavioral expectations established by the values and norms. The most basic condition of such compliance is the internalization of a society's values and norms by its members, for such socialization underlies the consensual basis of a societal community. In turn, socialization to the grounds of consensus is reinforced at various points by interlocking interests, notably economic and political. However, no society can maintain stability in the face of varying exigencies and strains unless the interest constellations of its members are grounded in solidarity and internalized loyalties and obligations.

Beyond consensus and the intermeshing of interests, there is still need for some machinery of *enforcement*. This need links in turn with the necessity for an authoritative interpretation of the institutionalized normative obligations. Hence, all societies have some type of "legal" procedures by which rights and wrongs can be decided without recourse to violence, and by which parties deemed in the wrong can be constrained from acting upon their interpretations, interests, or sentiments at the expense of others.

Because of the indicated territorial involvements of residence, work, religious activities, political organization, and various other factors, the maintenance of a normative order cannot be dissociated from control over activities within territorial areas. The function of government must include responsibility for preserving the *territorial integrity* of the society's normative order. This imperative has both an internal and an external reference. The first concerns the conditions of enforcing general norms and facilitating the performance of essential functions by the various units of the society. The second concerns the prevention of disruptive interference by non-members of the community. By virtue of the organic-locational exigencies we have discussed, the two references have one thing in common: The *ultimate preventive* of disruptive action is the use of physical force.[16] The use of force takes many forms, notably defense vis-à-vis outside territory and deprivation of liberty (imprisonment) within. The control or neutralization of the organized use of force is one functional necessity of maintaining a societal community. In more highly differentiated societies, this always involves some degree of governmental monopolization of socially organized force.

Thus a society's *primary* exigency vis-à-vis the personalities of its members is the motivation of their participation, including their compliance with the demands of its normative order. This exigency may be divided into three levels. First is the highly generalized commitment to the central value patterns that relate directly to the religious orientations. Second is the "sub-stratum" of the personality which, stemming from early socialization, links with the erotic complex and the motivational significance of kinship and other intimate rela-

[16] Parsons, "Some Reflections on the Place of Force in Social Process," *op. cit.*

tions. Third is the level more directly involved with services and the instrumental activities which vary with particular goals and situations. These levels of the personality correspond roughly to the superego, id, and ego in Freud's classification.

Secondarily, the linkage of the personality with the organism and the organism's involvement with the physical world operates in two relevant contexts which we have noted here. The first concerns the generalized organic processes that condition adequate personality functioning, especially in relation to the complexes of kinship, residence, and health. Second is the relation between coercion by physical force and the problem of maintaining the integrity of a societal normative order throughout a varied territory.

Organism and Physical Setting as Environment to Society

Consideration of the social system's relation to its organic base and, through that, to the physical world must begin with the physical requirements of organic life. Here the primordial problems concern the provision of food and shelter, but many other factors are also problematic in all known societies. Ramifying from the relatively simple tools and skills of primitive peoples to the very complex systems of modernity, technology is the socially organized capacity for actively controlling and altering objects of the physical environment in the interest of some human want or need. In limiting cases, the social organization may involve simply teaching skills to individual craftsmen who produce by themselves. But even in such cases, if the technology is important, the craftsman is unlikely to remain totally insulated from practitioners of his craft other than the master who taught him. Furthermore, if his work is specialized, he *must* have some organized relations with consumers of his product and, very likely, with sources of his materials and equipment. Truly, there can be no craft wholly divorced from social organization.

Technological processes obviously serve to meet human needs and wants. They depend on the cultural system for their *techniques*[17]—one person's addition to the total technical lore of his society is always an increment rather than an entirely "new system." Furthermore, technological tasks in this sense are always performed in a socially defined *role*. Products are very generally, though by no means always, the outcome of *collectively* organized processes, not the work of one individual. Thus some executive or coordinating functions must be performed in a broad variety of social relations with consumers, suppliers, workers, researchers, and the like.

Technology, then, is the primarily physical reference of the complex which includes the *economy* as its primary social system reference. The economy is the aspect of the societal system which functions not just to order technological procedures socially, but more importantly to fit them into the social system and control them in the interests of social units, whether individual or collective.[18] The institutional complexes of property, contract, and the regulation of terms of employment are important integrating elements here. The more strictly economic aspects of the complex are, in primitive and archaic societies, em-

[17] *Skill* is essentially the internalization of certain elements of culture in the *organism*.

[18] Talcott Parsons and Neil J. Smelser, *Economy and Society* (Glencoe, Ill.: The Free Press, 1956).

bedded in diffuse structures where kinship, religion, or political interests are paramount. Under certain circumstances, however, markets develop, along with money as a medium of exchange.

Technological organization, then, should be regarded as a boundary-structure between the society as a system and the organic-physical environment. On the societal side of the boundary, the economy is the focal structure, providing linkage with the societal community. Here, as the traditions of economic theory strongly emphasize, the function of *allocation* is central. Resources must be allocated toward the satisfaction of the vast variety of wants present in *any* society, and opportunities for satisfying wants must be allocated among different categories of the population. As socially organized, technological considerations also apply to the utilization of services. As the services of individuals become a truly mobile and *allocable* resource, they comprise an economic category, as their bracketing with physical goods in the economists' formula "goods and services" makes clear. Once involved (through employment) in an operating organization, however, they become engaged in what is in analytical terms political functioning—organizational processes oriented toward attaining the specific goals of the society or a relevant sub-collectivity.

These considerations imply that technology involves a complex of territorial references parallel to residence. In fact, it differentiates from the residence complex only late in social evolution.[19] Its major concern is the location of "industry." Insofar as personnel perform differentiated occupational or service roles, they must work *where* their services are needed, though this location must be coordinated with residential factors. However, location must also depend on access to materials and equipment and on distribution of output. Industry in the strict sense represents the case in which such economic considerations take primacy. But the location problems of governmental administration or of specialized religious personnel can be analyzed in somewhat similar terms.

The Societal Community and Self-Sufficiency

Certain priorities of control are inherent in the linkages between the societal sub-systems that relate the society to its environments and the societal community itself. The societal community is dependent on a superordinate *cultural* orientation system which is, above all, the primary source of legitimation for its normative order. This order then constitutes the most essential higher-order reference for the political and economic sub-systems, which connect most directly with the personality and organic-physical environments, respectively. In the political sphere, the priority of the societal normative order is highlighted most sharply in the function of enforcement[20] and in the need for agencies of the society to have some final control over sanctioning by

[19] Neil J. Smelser, *Social Change in the Industrial Revolution* (Chicago: University of Chicago Press, 1957).

[20] The emphasis on enforcement here is concerned with the conditions of security of a normative order. Where collective goal-attainment, as discussed above, is at issue, the corresponding emphasis will be on the effective mobilization of services and non-human resources. They are linked by the fact that adequate normative order in the political system is a condition of effective mobilization for goal-attainment.

physical force—not because physical force is the cybernetic controller, but because it must *be* controlled in order for the higher-order controls to operate. In the economic sphere, the parallel is that economic processes in the society (e.g., of allocation) must be institutionally controlled. Both cases also indicate the functional importance of *normative control* over the organism and the physical environment. When used as sanctions, force and other physical-organic factors contribute much more to the security of collective processes than they can as mere "conditional exigencies." Similarly, the priority of economic over technological considerations—questions of *what* is to be produced (and *for whom*) take precedence over questions of *how* things are to be produced—is a basic requirement for making technology actually useful.[21]

We may now sum up the ramifications of the self-sufficiency criterion we used in defining the concept of a society. A society must constitute a societal *community* that has an adequate level of integration or solidarity and a distinctive membership status. This does not preclude relations of control or symbiosis with population elements only partially integrated into the societal community, such as the Jews in the Diaspora, but there must be a core of more fully integrated members.

This community must be the "bearer" of a cultural system sufficiently generalized and integrated to legitimize a normative order. Such legitimation requires a system of constitutive symbolism which grounds the identity and solidarity of the community, as well as beliefs, rituals, and other cultural components which embody such symbolism. Cultural systems are usually broader than any one society and its community organization, although in areas containing many societies distinct cultural systems may indeed shade into one another. A society's self-sufficiency in this context, then, involves its institutionalizing a sufficient range of cultural components to meet its *societal* exigencies tolerably well. Of course, the relations among societies having the same or closely related cultural systems present special problems, some of which will be discussed later.

The element of collective organization imposes additional criteria of self-sufficiency. Self-sufficiency by no means requires that *all* the role-involvements of all members be carried on within the society. However, a society does have to provide a repertoire of role-opportunities sufficient for individuals to meet their fundamental personal exigencies at all stages of the life cycle without going outside the society, and for the society itself to meet its own exigencies. A celibate monastic order does not meet this criterion, because it cannot recruit new members by birth without violating its fundamental norms.

We have shown that the implementation of a normative order in a collectively organized population entails control over a territorial area. This is a very fundamental imperative regarding the integrity of governmental institutions. Furthermore, it is a major reason why no functionally specific collectivity such as a church or a business firm can be called a society. In relation to members as individuals, then, societal self-sufficiency requires—perhaps this is most fundamental—adequate control of motivational commitments. With exceptions

[21] Clearly, such priorities do not preclude two-way relations between the levels involved. Certainly a technological innovation leading to a new product can "stimulate" a demand for that product. But such a change always raises a new problem of allocation at the economic level: Is it justified in terms of alternative ways the relevant resources may be used?

which are inherently limiting (such as the establishment of new colonies), this requires that membership be recruited by birth and socialization, initially and primarily through a kinship system, however much it may be supplemented by formal education and other mechanisms. The recruitment complex may be considered a mechanism of social control over the personality structures of the membership.

Finally, self-sufficiency implies adequate control over the economic-technological complex so that the physical environment can be utilized as a resource base in a purposeful and balanced way. This control is intertwined with political control of territory and with control of membership in relation to the residence-kinship complex.

No one of these sub-criteria of self-sufficiency is paramount, except in regard to their generalized relations in the cybernetic and conditional hierarchies. Severe deficiency in any one or any combination of these criteria may be sufficient to destroy a society, or to create chronic instability or rigidity that prevents its further evolution. Hence this scheme will prove particularly useful in explaining breakdowns in the process of social evolution.

The Structural Components of Societies

The foregoing exposition of the relations between a society and its environment has employed a relatively systematic classification of structural components. It is important to make this scheme explicit because it underlies a great deal of the analysis in this book.

Our initial definition of the societal community focused on the interrelatedness of two factors—namely, a *normative order* and a *collectively* organized population. For most general purposes in analyzing societies, we need not extend our classification of components beyond a single distinction within each of these factors. We will distinguish between the aspects of each factor which are primarily internal to the societal community and those which primarily connect it with environing systems.

On the normative side, we can distinguish between *norms* and *values*. Values—in the pattern sense[22]—we regard as the primary connecting element between the social and cultural systems. Norms, however, are primarily social. They have regulatory significance for social processes and relationships but do not embody "principles" which are applicable beyond *social* organization, or often even a particular social system. In more advanced societies, the structural focus of norms is the legal system.

On the side of organized population, the *collectivity* is the category of intra-social structure and the *role* is the category of boundary-structure. The relevant boundary relation is with the personality of the individual member of the social system of reference. The boundary with the organic-physical complex is of an order that does not require distinct conceptualization in this context, although outputs from both personalities and the cultural system converge upon the organism in socialization processes, in the operation of skills, and in various other ways.

[22] It is important not to confuse this usage with the one referring to *valued objects*, which has been maintained by such theorists as Thomas and Znaniecki, Lasswell, Easton, and Homans.

These four structural categories—values, norms, collectivities, roles—may be related to our general functional paradigm.[23] Values take primacy in the pattern maintenance functioning of a social system. Norms are primarily integrative; they regulate the great variety of processes that contribute to the implementation of patterned value commitments. The primary functioning of the collectivity concerns actual goal attainment on behalf of the social system. Where individuals perform *societally* important functions, it is in their capacity as collectivity members. Finally, the primary function of the role in the social system is adaptive. This is particularly clear for the category of service, as the capacity to fulfill valued role-performances is the most basic generalized adaptive resource of any society, though it must be coordinated with cultural, organic, and physical resources.

Any concrete structural unit of a social system is always a combination of all four components—the present classification involves *components, not types*. We often speak of a role or collectivity as if it were a concrete entity, but this is, strictly speaking, elliptical. There is no collectivity without member roles and, vice-versa, no role which is not part of a collectivity. Nor is there a role or collectivity which is not "regulated" by norms and characterized by a commitment to value patterns. For analytical purposes we can, for example, abstract the value components from a structure and describe them as *cultural* objects, but when they are employed technically as categories of social structure they *always* refer to components of social systems which *also* contain all three of the other types of components.

Nevertheless, the four categories of components are, in the nature of the case, independently variable. Knowing the value pattern of a collectivity does not, for example, make it possible to deduce its role-composition. Cases in which the contents of two or more types of components vary together so that the content of one can be deduced directly from another are special and limiting, not general, cases.

Thus, the *same* value patterns generally form structural parts of a wide variety of different units or sub-systems in a society and are frequently found at many levels in structural hierarchies. Furthermore, the *same* norms are often essential to the functioning of a variety of kinds of operative units. Thus, the legal rights of property entail common normative elements whether the holder of such rights is a family, a religious body, or a commercial firm. Of course, norms are differentiated by situation and function, but the bases of their differentiation are never the same as those of collectivities and roles. Within limits, then, it appears that *any* collectivity involved in a certain situation or performing a certain function will be regulated by a certain norm *regardless* of its other features. Finally, such independent variation is also characteristic of roles. For example, executive or managerial roles and certain types of professional roles are common to many types of collectivity, not just one.

The same basic principle of independent variation applies to the relations between the social system and its environing systems. It is the person in role, not the total concrete individual, who is the member of a collectivity, even the societal community. For example, I am a member of certain international col-

[23] Cf. Talcott Parsons, "General Theory in Sociology," in Robert K. Merton, Leonard Broom, and Leonard S. Cottrell, Jr. (eds.), *Sociology Today* (New York: Basic Books, 1959, and Harper Torchbooks, 1965).

lectivities which are not parts of the American societal community. The plural character of the roles assumed by one personality is a major foundation of sociological theory and must be kept in mind continually. As a society evolves, role pluralism becomes more rather than less important, but it characterizes *any* society.

Process and Change

The phrase "Evolutionary and Comparative Perspectives" constitutes the subtitle of this book. The scheme of structural categories just outlined will provide the key references for the comparative aspect of our empirical analysis. Evolution, however, is a summary generalization standing for a type of process of change. Before proceeding to empirical matters, we must briefly consider the treatment of process, change, and the conception of societal evolution.

The type of process characteristic of social systems is what we call *interaction.*[24] To comprise action in our sense, such process must focus on *symbolic* levels. This means, essentially, the linguistic *level* of expression and communication—the conception of a broad level is justifiable because the factors we call speech and writing mesh with many other meaningful events, such as "gestures," physical "implementations" of goals, and so on. Furthermore, there are symbolic media of interaction other than language, such as money, which are probably better regarded as specialized languages than as essentially different orders of communication.

A language is not merely an aggregation of symbols which have been used in the past; it is a *system* of symbols which have meaning relative to a *code.*[25] A linguistic code is a *normative* structure parallel to that composed of societal values and norms—indeed, it is properly considered a special case of the norm if one allows for its cultural, as distinguished from a social, focus.

Processes of communication generally affect the recipients of messages, although the degree to which the effects are ones intended by the communicators is always problematical. The input of a message may stimulate an output which is in some sense a response. However, failure to respond is also an alternative, particularly if some messages are "broadcast" (e.g., printed in a newpaper), so that "anyone" may or may not notice and may or may not respond.

The process which leads to a response that is somehow related to one or more communicative inputs we may call a "decision." This process occurs inside that "black box," the personality of the actor. Insofar as the communication is part of a social process, the personality is acting *in a role,* the nature of which depends on his relations with the actual and potential recipients of the message and with sources from which communicative inputs are relayed to him.

Though a decision may ostensibly be a response to a particular message, it is elliptical to consider it the consequence of a single stimulus. A decision is *always* a consequence of a *combination* of factors, among which an immediate

[24] Parsons, "Interaction," *op. cit.*

[25] See Roman Jacobson and Morris Halle, *Fundamentals of Language* (The Hague: Mouton, 1956); and Noam Chomsky, *Syntactic Structures* (The Hague: Mouton, 1957).

input is only one. All social process must be conceived as the combination and re-combination of variable, communicable factors.

For example, the use of power can be conceived as the communication of a decision to the requisite parties, the implications of which bind a collectivity and the actions of its relevant members. Thus, in ordering his unit to carry out an attack, an officer merely gives the command, thereby activating a complex behavioral system on the part of his men. Clearly, however, such cybernetic *communicative processes* can operate effectively *only* in contexts in which *institutional structures* exercise tight cybernetic control over the various factors we discussed earlier.[26]

More detail on social processes will be introduced when particular examples in particular societies, or classes and systems of them, are discussed in subsequent chapters. The special type of process with which this book is concerned, however, is *change*. Though all processes change something, it is useful for our purposes to distinguish from others the processes which change social structures. Here, it is evident that many complex processes are necessary to *maintain* the functioning of any societal system; if its members never did anything, a society would very soon cease to exist.

At the most general theoretical levels, there is no difference between processes which serve to maintain a system and those which serve to change it. The difference lies in the intensity, distribution, and organization of the "elementary" components of particular processes relative to the states of the structures they affect. However, when we describe a charismatic revolution or the development of a bureaucratic system as processes, we are not speaking at such elementary levels, but are generalizing about very complex combinations of elementary processes. Of course, we will have to do this at many points, partly because space limitations preclude more detail, and partly because we lack knowledge about the finer composition of many of the processes in question.

A Paradigm of Evolutionary Change

Among change processes, the type most important to the evolutionary perspective is the *enhancement of adaptive capacity*, either within the society originating a new type of structure or, through cultural diffusion and the involvement of other factors in combination with the new type of structure, within other societies and perhaps at later periods. Some societies have been seedbeds of developments that became crucially important only long after the societies themselves ceased to exist. Ancient Israel and classical Greece did not endure long as distinct, politically independent societies, yet they contributed essential ingredients to the system of modern societies.

Nevertheless, both seedbed developments and cases of more immediate adaptive enhancement (such as the emergence of large-scale bureaucratic organizations in certain empires) seem capable of being analyzed in terms of a

[26] In two papers, I have developed this position to handle some much more complex problems in the conceptualization of social process; see "On the Concept of Influence," in *Public Opinion Quarterly* (Spring 1963) and "On the Concept of Political Power," in *Proceedings of the American Philosophical Society* (June 1963).

common paradigm, which I will simply sketch here, but elaborate further in subsequent chapters.

First is the process of *differentiation*. A unit, sub-system, or category of units or sub-systems having a single, relatively well-defined place in the society divides into units or systems (usually two) which differ in *both* structure and functional significance for the wider system. To take a familiar example already mentioned, the kinship-organized household in predominantly peasant societies is *both* the unit of residence and the primary unit of agricultural production. In certain societies, however, most productive work is performed in specialized units, such as workshops, factories, or offices manned by people who are *also* members of family households. Thus two sets of roles and collectivities have become differentiated, and their functions separated. There must also be some differentiation at the level of norms and some specification of common value patterns to the different situations.

If differentiation is to yield a balanced, more evolved system, each newly differentiated sub-structure (e.g., the producing organization in the above case) must have increased adaptive capacity for performing its *primary* function, as compared to the performance of *that* function in the previous, more diffuse structure. Thus economic production is typically more efficient in factories than in households. We may call this process the *adaptive upgrading* aspect of the evolutionary change cycle. It applies to both role and collectivity levels; the participating people, as well as the collectivity as a whole, must become more productive than before, as measured by some kind of output-cost relationship. These changes do not imply that the older "residual" unit will have "lost function" in all contexts of its operations. The household is no longer an important economic producer, but it may well perform its other functions better than in its earlier form.

Differentiation processes also pose new problems of *integration* for the system. The operations of two (or more) categories of structural units must be coordinated where only one category existed before. Thus, in employment-occupational systems, the father of the household can no longer supervise production *in his kinship role*. Therefore, the producing organization must develop an authority system which is *not* embedded in kinship, and the producing and household collectivities must be coordinated within the broader system—e.g., through changes in the structure of the local community.

Adaptive upgrading thus requires that specialized functional capacities be freed from ascription within more diffuse structural units. There is, then, a reliance upon more *generalized* resources that are independent of their ascriptive sources. For these reasons, differentiation and upgrading processes may require the *inclusion* in a status of full membership in the relevant general community system of previously excluded groups which have developed legitimate capacities to "contribute" to the functioning of the system.[27] Perhaps the most common case concerns systems which have been divided into superior and inferior classes, and in which the upper class has monopolized the status of "real" membership, treating the lower class, so far as it is conceived to belong at all, as a second-class citizenry. The processes of differentiation and upgrading make it increasingly difficult to maintain such simple dichotomies. Differentiation, particularly,

[27] This may be a case of extending the scope of community to avoid the expulsion of newly differentiated elements—e.g., cadet lineages with new residential locations.

As the above outline of inter-system relations shows, we would expect this process of differentiation at the level of the general action system to stimulate, and be stimulated by, similar processes internal to the society as a system.

What we call the pattern-maintenance system of the society has *cultural* primacy in that it is the locus of direct relationship with the cultural system. It first becomes clearly differentiated from the other societal sub-systems as the latter establish themselves as clearly "secular" spheres which, though legitimized in religious terms, are not directly part of the religious system. This process leads to the differentiation of "church and state," which was not fully achieved until the post-Roman phases of Christianity.

The development of autonomous legal systems is perhaps the most important indicator of differentiation between the societal integrative system, focusing about the societal community, and the polity, which is concerned with the selection, ordering, and attainment of collective goals rather than the maintenance of solidarity (including order) as such. Of all pre-modern systems, Roman society made the greatest progress in this direction.

Finally, the economy tends to become differentiated, not only from technology, but also from the polity and those aspects of pattern-maintenance associated with kinship. Money and markets are among the most important institutional complexes involved in the differentiation of the economy. Perhaps the differences between Mesopotamian and Greek society mark the most crucial earlier steps in this institutional development, but many additional developments occurred in the transition to modern systems.

The master scheme of four functions and our analysis of the tendency of societal systems to differentiate into four *primary* sub-systems will constitute major guidelines for our whole analysis.[31] Where there appear to be more than four important sub-systems, we will treat this in one or a combination of three ways. First, the essential phenomenon may be due to segmentation rather than differentiation. Second, more than one level of system-reference may be involved. For example, kinship institutions involve a special integration between societal components located in the pattern-maintenance sub-system and personality, and are hence functionally less differentiated than such structures as modern universities or churches. Third, there are different distributions of primacy among functionally significant components, so that important typological distinctions must be made *within* a relatively highly differentiated sub-system—e.g., an economy or polity. Often these differences result from interpenetrations with elements at other system levels or other sub-systems at the same level.

Hence, it should be clear that the grounding of the above classification is analytical, not concrete.[32] Any particular sub-system of a society may involve all three types of complication in a special combination. It is, however, important for theoretical purposes to disentangle them analytically. Although the concrete specifics will vary considerably (and complexly) according to the type of system we are analyzing, the reference points of the societal sub-systems—pattern-maintenance, integration, polity, and economy—will comprise a major analytical tool of our entire analysis.

[31] Cf. Parsons, Part II of the "General Introduction" to *Theories of Society, op. cit.*

[32] That is, it follows from the theoretical relations depicted in Table 2, especially in columns I, II, III.

Stages in the Evolution of Societies

An evolutionary perspective implies both a criterion of evolutionary direction and an evolutionary scheme of stages. We have formulated the directional factor as an increase in generalized adaptive capacity consciously adapting it from the theory of organic evolution. It will be further interpreted in our concluding chapter.

Here it remains to address the problem of stages. We do not conceive societal evolution to be either a continuous or a simple linear process, but we can distinguish between broad levels of advancement without overlooking the considerable variability found in each. For the limited purposes of this book and its sequel, we will distinguish three very broad evolutionary levels, which we will call *primitive, intermediate,* and *modern.* This book will focus upon the first two categories, leaving the third for the sequel. There is some arbitrariness in any particular scheme of stages, and within the two broad categories to be treated below, we will find it essential to make a major sub-division within each.[33]

The dividing criteria, or watersheds, between the major stages in our classification center about critical developments in the code elements of the normative structures. For the transition from primitive to intermediate society, the focal development is in language, which is primarily part of the cultural system. In the transition from intermediate to modern society, it is in the institutionalized codes of normative order internal to the societal structure and centers in the legal system.

In both cases, the criterion stated is merely a catch-word indicating a complex subject matter. *Written language,* the focus of the fateful development out of primitiveness, increases the basic differentiation between the social and cultural systems and vastly extends the range and power of the latter. The principal symbolic contents of a culture can, with writing, be embodied in forms which are independent of concrete interaction contexts. This makes possible an immensely wider and more intensive cultural diffusion, both in space (e.g., relative to populations) and in time. It initiates the phenomenon of "broadcasting"—i.e., the orientation of messages to undefined audiences, to whomever is literate in the language and comes across the document. Furthermore, there is no inherent time limitation on the relevance of a message. Only literate cultures can have a *history* in the sense of an awareness, based on documentary evidence, of past events which are beyond the memories of living persons and the vague hearsay of oral traditions.

There are many aspects and stages of the development and institutionalization of written language and literacy.[34] The early stages, particularly prominent in what we call archaic societies, generally confine writing to the "craft" literacy of small groups using it for specialized purposes, often esoterically religious and magical. A second important development, probably a criterion of the advanced intermediate society, is the institutionalization of full literacy for

[33] Bellah, in his notable article, "Religious Evolution," uses a scheme of five major stages, which does not exactly correspond with the present scheme. Partly, we have different perspectives, Bellah's being more specifically upon cultural than societal factors. But I think our differing schemes also involve a difference of theoretical opinion.

[34] Cf. Jack Goody and Ian Watt, "The Consequences of Literacy," in *Comparative Studies in Society and History* (April 1963).

the adult males of an upper class. Such societies usually organize their cultures about a set of especially important, usually sacred, writings, knowledge of which is expected of all "educated" men. Only modern societies approach institutionalizing literacy for the whole adult population, which indeed may signalize a second major stage of modernity.

Written language and the availability of documents act to stabilize a great many social relations. For example, the terms of a contractual agreement need not depend on the fallible memories of the parties or witnesses but can be written and made available for verification as need arises. The importance of such stability should not be underestimated. Undoubtedly, it is a major condition for increasing the extent and complexity of many components of social organization.

At the same time, writing is also a source of flexibility and an opportunity for innovation. However frequently "classical" documents have provided the basis for a rigid traditionalism, the availability of officially correct documents makes possible a much more far-reaching and deep-going critical analysis of relevant cultural issues. If the document is normative for some sphere of action, it poses quite acutely the problem of how, in practical situations, its injunctions may actually be fulfilled. Above all, written documents form a basis for a *cumulative* cultural development; they permit the *differences* introduced by an innovation to be defined far more precisely than by oral tradition alone.

While written language furthers the *independence* of the cultural system from the more conditional exigencies of the society, law, when developed to the requisite level, furthers the independence of the normative components of the societal structure from the exigencies of political and economic interests and from the personal, organic, and physical-environmental factors operating through them.

The problem concerning the kind of law, the institutionalization of which marks the transition from intermediate to modern societies, is highly complex. Clearly, its organization must be highly generalized according to universalistic principles. It is this factor, above all, that precludes such imposing systems as the Talmudic law, or that of traditional Islam, from being classed as "modern" law. They lack the level of generality which Weber called *formal rationality*.[35] Modern legal systems must also strongly emphasize the factor of *procedure*, as distinguished from substantive precepts and standards. Only on the basis of procedural primacy can the system cope with a wide variety of changing circumstances and types of cases without prior commitment to specific solutions.

As we shall see, Roman law of the Imperial period came by far the closest, among pre-modern systems, to meeting the more "formal" aspects of these requirements—and, of course, it made essential contributions to the later emergence of fully modern systems. However, it was not a sufficient framework for developing "modern" structures in the Roman Empire itself. We will suggest that this was primarily due to the level of the institutionalization of law in Roman society. The Roman Empire did not develop a sufficiently integrated societal community, and failed to integrate all the major ethnic, territorial, and religious groups with reference to a single primary normative order standing for the whole society and above the authority of Roman government.

[35] Cf. Max Rheinstein (ed.), *Max Weber on Law in Economy and Society* (Cambridge: Harvard University Press, 1954), especially Chap. 8.

Table 1

Sub-systems of Action

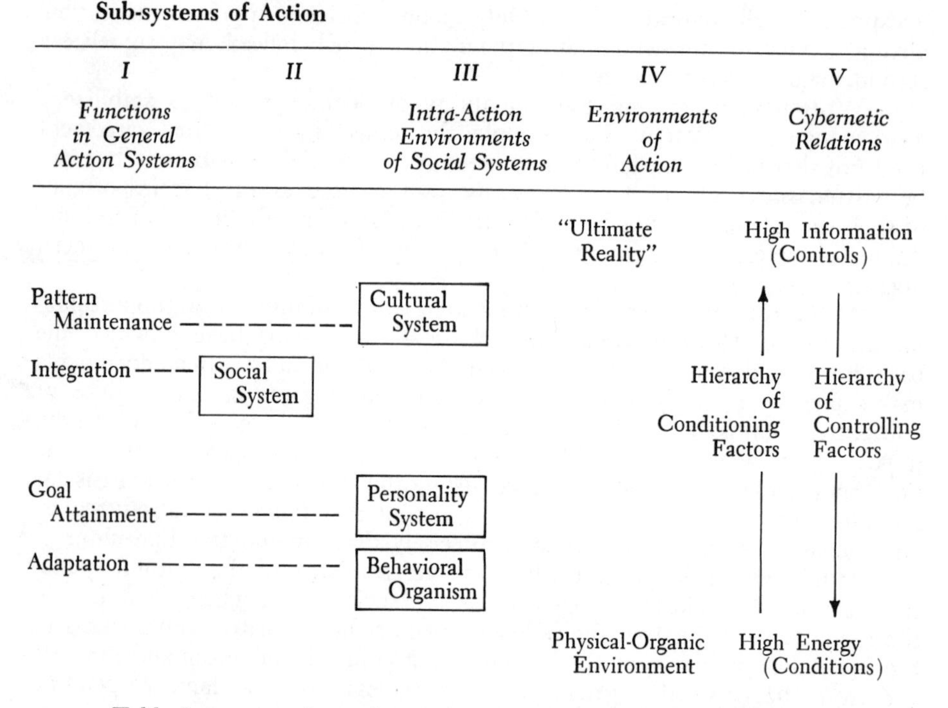

Table 1 presents the main relations between the social system and its total system of environments in terms of the functional scheme we have used. Column I lists the functional categories, interpreted here at the general action level. Column II singles out the social system from the others according to its integrative functions within the action system. Column III, corresponding to Column IV of Table 2, lists the other three primary sub-systems of action as immediate (i.e., as intra-action) environments of the social system. Column IV presents the two environments within which action systems function—at least so far as they are distinguished here—namely, the physical-organic environment, relations with which are mediated in the first instance through the behavioral organism, and the environment we have called "ultimate reality," relations with which are mediated through the constitutive symbol systems (i.e., religious components) of the cultural system. Finally, Column V indicates the two directions in which factors exert their effect on these systems. The upward-pointed arrow indicates the hierarchy of conditions, which at any given cumulative level in the upward series is, in the common formula, "necessary but not sufficient." The downward-pointed arrow designates the hierarchy of controlling factors, in the cybernetic sense. As we move downward, control of more and more necessary conditions makes the implementation of patterns, plans, or programs possible. Systems higher in the order are relatively high in information while those lower down are relatively high in energy.

Table 2

The Societal Community and Its Environments

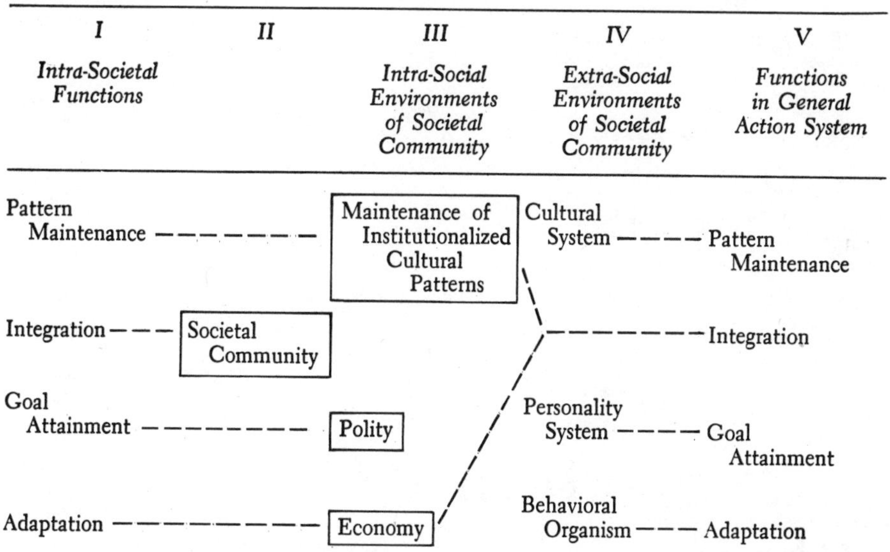

I	II	III	IV	V
Intra-Societal Functions		*Intra-Social Environments of Societal Community*	*Extra-Social Environments of Societal Community*	*Functions in General Action System*
Pattern Maintenance		Maintenance of Institutionalized Cultural Patterns	Cultural System	Pattern Maintenance
Integration	Societal Community			Integration
Goal Attainment		Polity	Personality System	Goal Attainment
Adaptation		Economy	Behavioral Organism	Adaptation

Table 2 presents schematically the set of relationships which have been outlined in the text concerning the primary structure of the society as a system, centering on the place of the societal community. Column I lists the four primary functional categories according to their place in the cybernetic hierarchy of control. In relation to column I, column II identifies the societal community as the integrative sub-system of the society—i.e., that *analytically* defined sub-system characterized by the primacy of integrative function in the larger system. Column III designates the other three primary analytical sub-systems (the functions of which are also given in relation to column I) as constituting environments of the societal community which are *internal* to the society as a social system. It both carries on processes of input-output interchange and shares certain zones of interpenetration with them. Column IV details in the cognate order the primary sub-systems of action other than the social system itself, showing them as in turn constituting environments for the social system, presuming the same order of interchange and interpenetration, but with different specific content. The slanting dashed lines indicate that the *entire* societal system, not each of its sub-systems, is involved in these interchanges with the action environments. Finally, Column V lists the functional categories in terms of which action systems are differentiated, this time in the context of the general action system rather than, as in Column I, of the social system.

three

primitive societies

In the last chapter, we designated the institutionalization of written language in the culture of an upper class as the "watershed" between primitive and intermediate societies. Short of fulfilling this criterion, societies may range immensely in type and in mode of development. The present chapter presents a brief treatment of this range of variation and development.

The gap between man and the other species, though redefined since Darwin, remains crucial. Man is the only *cultural* animal and his culture, being fundamentally interdependent with his society, makes his social organization very different from that of other species; e.g., the social insects or even other primates. Clearly, a process of organic evolution crossed this gap at least once. However, its final stages so enhanced adaptation that species intermediate between the higher primates and man could not stabilize viable "niches" in the organic world and were eliminated by natural selection. Hence, an extremely laborious reconstruction—still very incomplete—has been necessary to conceptualize them.

In general, the distinctively human organic developments ground the capacities which underlie cultural-social life and organization, which are primarily capacities for "learning" and for utilizing and organizing learned materals and patterns. They comprise the essential conditions for organizing behavior in terms of symbolic systems, which is what constitutes *action* in our technical sense. In the realm of action, the gene has been replaced by the symbol as the basic structural element.[1]

The oldest of these organic developments seems to have been the emer-

[1] Alfred Emerson, "Homeostasis and Comparison of Systems," in Roy R. Grinker (ed.), *Toward A Unified Theory of Behavior* (New York: Basic Books, 1956).

gence of arms and hands as manipulative organs.[2] Having two hands, each located at the end of a movable jointed arm, and each with four fingers and an opposable thumb, man has a general purpose "tool" which is immensely superior to any mouth-and-paws combination. It entails erect posture, and hence a considerable sacrifice in effective locomotion—no human runner matches a horse in speed. But the hands are the primary basis of what we call human skills.

Skills constitute the manipulative techniques of human goal attainment and control in relation to the physical world, so far as artifacts or machines especially designed as tools do not yet supplement them. Truly human skills are guided by organized and codified *knowledge* of both the things to be manipulated and the human capacities that are used to manipulate them. Such knowledge is an aspect of cultural-level symbolic processes, and, like other aspects to be discussed presently, requires the capacities of the human central nervous system, particularly the brain. This organic system is clearly essential to all of the symbolic processes; as we well know, the human brain is far superior to the brain of any other species.[3]

The most general aspect of the symbolic process is language, the primary organic implementation of which is speech. Speech involves an especially interesting "secondary" utilization of the oral organs, some of which originally evolved in relation to food intake and respiration. The hollow throat chamber (its air flow controlled by breathing and by opening and closing the mouth and its shape controlled by movements of the lips, cheeks, and tongue) combined with the vocal chords (which provide reverberations) can flexibly produce extremely varied and controlled sounds. Since human manual skills permit the mouth merely to receive and masticate food, instead of having also to grasp and tear it, the oral organs have presumably become specialized around such flexibility. A brain which can control this apparatus and an aural system with which the brain can decode the sound-speech information transmitted to the organism make linguistic symbolic communication possible.

Another organic complex is especially significant for learning itself. The prolonged dependence of offspring on parents is a major characteristic of the more advanced species. Humans not only follow the general mammalian pattern of gestating in the maternal body and depending on maternal feeding, but also exhibit the trait—present in lower primates, but immensely accentuated in man—of *psychological* dependence on an older, nurturing organism.[4] In this context, as well as that of physiological reproduction, the family is complexly and variously foreshadowed at pre-human levels, but the human emphasis on the *continuing* care of young offspring is quite unique, not only organically through feeding and protection, but especially in psychological terms.[5]

Since Freud, it has become well understood that the *erotic complex* (as it is better called than by Freud's earlier term "sexual") plays a special role in the control of learning processes. Its essential organic mechanism is the capacity to

[2] Ernst Mayr, *Animal Species and Evolution* (Cambridge: Harvard University Press, 1963), Chap. 20.

[3] Ralph W. Gerard, "Brains and Behavior," in J. N. Spuhler (ed.), *The Evolution of Man's Capacity for Culture* (Detroit: Wayne State University Press, 1957).

[4] Harry F. Harlow, "Basic Social Capacity of Primates," in Spuhler (ed.), *op. cit.*

[5] Mayr, *op. cit.*

be motivated by erotic pleasure. In learning a whole series of early disciplines, the human infant finds that contacts with the mother are pleasurable and that, within the context of his relationship with her, they reward his learning. These disciplines including feeding skills, sleeping and waking routines, toilet-training, and even language-learning. The internalization and organization at the symbolic level of the erotic significance of social objects underlies the learning of more complicated disciplines and eventually the erotic complex of adulthood. In the psychological-motivational contexts, the erotic complex seems to be the most essential bridge between the organic and action system levels.

These classes of organic capacity seem to be most essential to a human individual's acquisition and use of culture, in his interaction with others, and in the formation of his own personality. They exhibit in common the basic property often called *plasticity*. On one level, they are all *genetically* determined—*any* normal human organism will develop them in adequate degree under normal conditions. They are, however, simply *capacities*. Their organic foundations do not determine the actual content of the general behavioral patternings which their "utilization" makes possible. Having hands and arms and good coordination are necessary conditions for acquiring manual skills, but they in no way determine *what* skills will be acquired. Having a properly functioning brain is essential to any high intellectual achievement, but does not determine whether the "learning" will involve philosophy, mathematics, or biology, or Christian, Buddhist, or Confucian beliefs. An adequate vocal apparatus is necessary to speak a language, but has nothing to do with what particular language is learned. Erotic capacities are essential for psycho-sexual development, but there is no evidence that the different patternings of Australian aboriginal psycho-sexual development and modern European psycho-sexual development are related to the genetic differences between the respective "races."

Thus, the *organization* of action systems as a whole is learned, but is based on a set of *generalized* organic facilities, the common availability of which is the most distinctive genetic heritage of human beings. The ways in which they are used—and are built into cultures, social systems, and personalities at the human action level—are independent of *any* genetic particularities of the particular organic stock. This is the view of the organic bases of human behavior which modern biological and social science has substituted for the "instinct" theories that held sway during the early part of this century.[6]

The Components of Primitive Society

All these organic components may be involved in *all* types of human socio-cultural behavior, though in differing patterns of combination and relative importance. Hence, there is no simple, one-to-one correspondence between these components and the institutional complexes of even the most primitive human societies. However, there are always patterns of special relevance—e.g., manual skills are particularly important in technological adaptation and the organization of erotic relations is particularly important in contexts of kinship and the socialization of children.

[6] It is particularly unfortunate that Freud's term *trieb*, which was neutral between these different views, has been translated into English as *instinct*. As Freud made progressively more clear, the erotic complex is a *generalized* capacity to mobilize the organic components of motivation to action, not a "propensity" to highly specific modes of behavior.

Just as the organic components all exhibit plasticity, so the socio-cultural components of behavior are all *organized* on symbolic bases. For example, in the areas of action which contemporary ideologies most often "reduce" to the operation of organic factors, technology and "sex," we strenuously oppose the idea that *any* patterned human behavior can be understood as purely organic rather than as controlled by socio-cultural mechanisms. Doubtless, food-getting and eating are subject to the nutritional imperatives of organic life and are in some sense motivated by the hunger drive, but, beyond their obvious *conditional* relevance, these factors can *never* fully account for human *ways* of securing and eating food. Similarly, though sexual intercourse is normally essential for human reproduction and there is an organic factor in sexual desire, the patternings of erotic relations in human societies are *never* understandable as simple functions of this organic "need." In particular, the connections between the erotic relations of adults, and parenthood and the socialization of children are always fundamentally important.

Insofar as an action system is highly primitive in the sense mentioned in the last chapter, it will be highly *undifferentiated* at the social, cultural, and personality levels. Its societal system will be of the most simple type by the standards of differentiation which we will apply throughout this book. At the same time, there will be relatively little differentiation between the societal and the other components of the action system. "Society" and "cultural system" do not have very generalized bases for keeping independent of each other; "society" and "personality" have characteristic modes by which their structures fuse at the more generalized levels. It may even be difficult to distinguish adjacent societies from one another, for some primitive societies are not clearly bounded either in territory or in membership in the sense that more advanced societies are.

Two formulas are commonly put forward as criteria of societal primitiveness. One is the overwhelming importance in all spheres of action of religious (and magical) orientations to the world. The other is the prominence of kinship relations; it is often said that kinship structures are a factor in practically all social organization in primitive systems.[7] But considerable attention has also been given to two other complexes—namely, technology and the symbolic nature of social communication. Perhaps we can reformulate these four complexes (religion, kinship, technology, and symbolic communication) as analytically defined components of a primitive societal system, relating them here to the exigencies of functioning in primitive societies and later to developmental trends toward more complex societies.[8]

First is a system of *constitutive symbolism*, which gives members of the society their own self-definition, or collective identity, so that the conception, "We, the . . . ." is meaningful. This is a kind of answer to the two questions of who and what *we* are.[9]

This system of symbolism always links in some way with the kinship system. Often this connection is grounded in an ancestral reference to those

[7] Claude Levi-Strauss, *Totemism* (Boston: Beacon Paperbacks, 1962), especially Chap. II.

[8] Cf. Parsons, "Evolutionary Universals in Society," *op. cit.*

[9] Emile Durkheim and Marcel Mauss, *Primitive Classification* (Chicago: University of Chicago Press, 1963).

from whom *we* are descended and a conception of a transition from clearly human ancestors to those conceived as being supernatural. The latter are then regarded as the original founders of the society, and the normative order is believed to have been established by their actions and/or decrees. For example, it is a common belief among primitive societies that the founders had incestuous relations but decreed that their human descendants should be forbidden them. The principal framework of the kinship system is usually explained by such foundation myths.

In such cases, the humanness of the founding ancestors is equivocal in two directions. In the supernatural direction, for example, they are regarded as immortal and as possessing various other supernatural powers. In the opposite direction, however, the ancestors tend to become "sub-humanized" and are portrayed as or associated with animals or perhaps plants or physical objects. Totemism is a very common phenomenon here, but there may also be more generally significant "superanimals," such as the serpent *Yu* (*Yurlunggur* or *Wollunqua*) of Murngin myth.[10] These are clearly symbols that operate in a variety of contexts.

Finally, there is always a territorial reference, including the country in which the people live, sometimes complicated by tales of migration. It includes conceptions of their hunting, gathering, and residence areas, and of special locations that have a sacred significance, such as the water holes from which ancestors are thought to have emerged in Australia.

Thus, the constitutive symbolism gives meaning to, and integrates the meaning of, the principal components of the human condition in their salience to the group in question. It includes symbolization of organic life, as limited by birth and death; of the physical environment and the exigencies of living, including territory; of the social statuses of men and their involvements with reproduction and biological descent; and of the modes of social communication, especially through language. It is the original boundary structure between the cultural and social systems in primitive societies.

Constitutive symbolism becomes engaged in social processes through its inclusion in a more comprehensive system of communicative codes, which is at once normative and operative. This system contains a set of rules regulating the interactions of people in such situations as marriages, inter-generational relations, subsistence technology, and relations to sacred entities, in terms of the symbolic meanings of their specific social statuses. Language in a technical sense seems to be a crucial part of this communication complex, as it enables analytically and symbolically formulated information to be conveyed among persons. Along with the common meanings embodied in the constitutive symbolism, what brings a people together as a society is, above all, a common system of "operative" codes which regulate their communications with one another. Like the system of constitutive symbolism, such codes must articulate with all the principal contexts of the human condition, technological, social, moral, religious, and so on. Within the societal system, however, there must be a code system which regulates the processes of communicating and acting on information specifically in terms of the *social statuses* of the actors involved. For example, within a given type of social situation people of a certain social status are to be

[10] W. Lloyd Warner, *A Black Civilization*, 2nd ed. (New York: Harper, 1958), Chaps. IX and X.

believed or obeyed more than people of other statuses. Regulations of this type, when organized into highly ramified systems, allocate very complex and generalized properties of influence to the statuses—especially the "high" ones—within the society. In advanced societies, there is provision for the fulfillment of commitments, the exercise of power, and the expenditure of money under regulations that assure the relative structural independence of these processes from the use of influence. The system of regulations must be highly differentiated in these cases, however, in order to link the various modes of social communication with the appropriate statuses and situations. In primitive societies, the generalized standards by which the codes are organized tend to be highly undifferentiated. The modes of communication are deeply intertwined, can be exercised only in very stereotyped fashion, and are tightly controlled by the various exigencies of social solidarity. In the broadest sense, the code system is the "law" of a society, even the most primitive.[11] Among the components of primitive societies, it has the most direct reference to the internal maintenance of societal solidarity and is the farthest removed from the boundaries with the non-social subsystems of action.

Constitutive symbol systems and their associated codes, then, order the relations among the individuals and social groups that comprise a population. In the first instance, however, the population is established in terms of its kinship organization. At the mammalian level, it is clear that the complex of biological reproduction, hence of filiation, socialization, and selection of those who will join in reproduction, constitutes the conditional focus of the *genesis* of solidary groups within the population of a species. But, to quote Durkheim, a *society* (especially a primitive one) constitutes "a moral community called a church"; the basis of *societal* solidarity is not "primordial" in the sense of inhering either *in* discrete kinship units or in "biological" principles of their organization. Only on a basis which morally integrates an extended, complex set of kinship units can a population take the step from primordial solidarity to societal solidarity.[12] This is what we mean in speaking of a kinship *system*, a concept with an essentially societal reference. However, in its general functioning, kinship is the major type of boundary structure between the social and personality systems by virtue of its "primordial" involvements.

Physical skills, related to a cultural technology and the population's control of its physical environment, constitute the fourth basic component of primitive action systems, as they are institutionalized in a division of labor and patterns of cooperation, and allocation of resources. Particularly in the economic situations within which they are most salient, they structure the boundary between the society and the behavioral organism.

The Primitive Society of Aboriginal Australia

The societies of aboriginal Australia probably provide the best example for a first illustration of primitive societal organization, for

[11] Cf. Marcel Mauss, *The Gift* (London: Cohen and West, 1954). Noam Chomsky, *Syntactic Structures* (The Hague: Mouton, 1953).

[12] Emile Durkheim, *The Elementary Forms of the Religious Life* (London: Allen and Unwin, 1915); Cf. Rodney Needham, *Structure and Sentiment* (Chicago: University of Chicago Press, 1960.)

they are among the most primitive societies known and have been rather thoroughly studied by both field observers and theorists.

The social organization of the Australians can be described almost wholly in terms of the kinship system and its complex articulations with the totemic cults, the circulating rights and obligations of solidary relationships, and ways of controlling the environment.[13] The economy is of the simplest sort, resting on hunting and the gathering of berries, roots, and certain edible insects. It requires that the bands (generally composed of patrilineal kin) range over considerable territory. The normative order has definite territorial references in that there are traditionally established areas within which specific kin groups are conventionally entitled to hunt and gather. However, considerable and varying numbers of such independent bands get together for special ceremonial occasions.

Not only is kinship central to the social organization, but there is relatively little differentiation among the basic kinship units; [14] no set of clans occupies a generally superior status, with special political authority, religious preferment, or access to wealth. Furthermore, kinship statuses are major components of practically all social roles.

Given the incest taboo, kinship systems are organized on the double basis of descent and affinity (relationship established by marriage). The child is "located" in the society by virtue of his parentage—as is the case in all societies, with only a few, clearly marginal exceptions. In very primitive societies, however, such "location" is extremely diffuse, as practically all of an individual's privileges and obligations tend to be *prescribed* in terms of his kinship status, especially his affiliation with his kinship group. Perhaps the major problem for such prescriptive systems arises from the fact that marriage, because of the incest taboo, necessarily involves relations with units outside the primary descent group. Nevertheless, marriage choice may be prescribed in terms of kinship categories; the descent group to which a person belongs may have institutionalized relations with other descent groups which rigidly prescribe the groups into which he (or she) may and may not marry.[15] The situation contrasts sharply with that obtaining in modern societies, in which all opposite-sex members are eligible for marriage except limited categories of close relatives.

In such primitive systems, the *whole society* constitutes a *single affinal collectivity*, or union of descent groups allied through the marriages of their members. Descent and marriage are so linked that those who belong in specific descent groups not only can but *must* marry persons belonging to specific other descent groups. Hence, the society consists of an intricate network of groupings composed by variations on the themes of descent, sex, and age-grouping. These groupings are interrelated by the principle of cross-cousin marriage. This defines the marriage obligation in a way which makes eligible the "closest" type of same generation relative outside the nuclear family and descent group of birth. However, the prescriptive rules, operating along generation lines, establish the categorical equivalence of same-sex generation-mates of a descent group. In terms of the general structure of the kinship system, it seems not to matter

[13] Levi-Strauss, *op. cit.*

[14] Warner, *op. cit.*, Chap. I.

[15] Claude Levi-Strauss, *Les Structures Elèmentaires de La Parentè* (Paris: Presses Universitaires 1949); Needham, *op. cit.*

which particular person is chosen as a marriage partner, so long as he or she falls in the proper kinship category—a category which equally includes all the collaterals from the proper type of first cousin "outward" to more "distant" relatives, even though anthropologists commonly call it by the type of first cousin involved.[16]

The Australian tribes vary between those in which the eligible *categories* of marriage partner (for a male) are at the same time "mother's brother's daughters" and "father's sister's daughters," and those in which the cross-cousin prescription is unilateral (i.e., from the viewpoint of a certain group, the groups to which women are given as wives are distinguished from those which give women as wives) and descent must be reckoned through several lines. Thus, the Murngin seem to have twelve descent categories, while the Arunta distinguish only two.[17] All types of these systems involve a complex geometry of marriage and descent groups, the analysis of which has generated considerable controversy among anthropologists. The underlying common principle, however, is prescription of marriage by kinship category. Though specific systems may vary considerably with differing conditions, the general *kind* of system is a direct outcome of this principle.[18]

Certain societies exhibit a particularly interesting consequence of such categorization of marriage prescription. While the "inside" limit of eligibility is clearly defined by the prohibition on brother-sister marriage, the outside boundary may be left undefined. Although the whole society constitutes an affinal collectivity, there is sometimes no precise way of defining who are (and are not) members of the societal community on the outer fringes of the kinship network. For example, all fellow-Murngin are relatives, but from any band-centered perspective, the boundary between Murngin and non-Murngin is unclear. Furthermore, this kinship unboundedness seems also to apply to religion and the communicative code system. There are bases, especially territorial and religious, on which the "seamless web" of particularistic kinship and totemic ties becomes so attenuated that relationships are no longer effective. However, it seems that the aborigines have foregone clarity of societal boundedness as a feature of their adaptation to the Australian environment and their common situation of being surrounded by groups quite similar in cultural and social characteristics. It is clear that such unboundedness is not characteristic of all very primitive societies—certainly all have scant capacity to ensure their boundaries (e.g., against invasion), but only some of them seem to institutionalize positive unboundedness. Yet it is also clear that no society could attain what we will call the "advanced primitive" level of societal evolution without developing

[16] *Ibid.*

[17] *Ibid.* Cf. Edmund Leach, "The Structural Implications of Matrilateral Cross-Cousin Marriage," in his *Rethinking Anthropology* (London: Athlone Press, 1961).

[18] One might allege that the structural intricacy of Australian kinship systems conflicts with the assertion that Australian society is highly undifferentiated. However, our proposition relates to the differentiation of other functional categories of social structure *from* the kinship nexus—e.g., political, economic, legal, religious. This is a different problem from that of the internal differentiation of any one of these sub-systems of a society. The tendency toward the pattern of the isolated nuclear family in modern societies greatly reduces the complexity of the kinship system relative to primitive cases. However, it is precisely this that increases the differentiation from the kinship system of the other sectors of the society and that makes possible (indeed, makes necessary) their integration in terms of a more generalized societal code and underlying cultural system.

relatively clear-cut boundedness. Thus, a lack of boundedness seems to be an important mark of a society's primitiveness.

The rigidity of prescription that is so striking in Australian kinship evidently involves the relative brittleness of the institutional safeguards against reversion to sub-human levels of motivational organization, as it would affect the maintenance of a solidary societal community. Here the focus is the problem of incest and these societies' distinctively prominent elaboration of precautions against incestuous marriages.[19]

As we mentioned, aboriginal Australian economic organization is extremely simple, consisting of hunting and gathering in a somewhat difficult environment. It, too, is closely ascribed to the kinship system; one performs specific technological-economic functions by virtue of one's specific kinship status, including sex. This is a most important point. Along with various strictly technological measures, such as control of fire and the production and use of simple tools, the distinctively human economic characteristic of these societies, as compared to primate groups, is the *flexible social organization* of technological-economic functions. This includes institutionalization of division of labor (notably between the sexes), the cooperative organization of activities (as in hunting), and the allocation of resources among specified kin groups.[20] Perhaps there are closer analogies with sub-human groups in the technological-economic sphere than in the others, but, more broadly, its integration with kinship, religion, and the communication codes is an unmistakably human breakthrough.

Durkheim particularly emphasized and documented the "pan-religionism" of the most primitive societies. He stressed, despite the distinctiveness of the profane sphere (or aspect) of activities, the striking extent to which a primitive society as a whole is permeated with religious sentiments and activities. This includes not only the prominence of religio-magical belief systems and the prevalence of ritual activities, but also the striking emotional excitement which pervades so much of the religious sphere.[21]

We may use Durkheim's words and speak of the prominent *order* of *sacred* things in Australian society. Like kinship, it is not only prominent, but also elaborately structured. This elaboration, too, apparently relates closely to the prescriptiveness of the whole socio-cultural system and is perhaps most evident in the sacred order's ties to the kinship system. There are no independent "cults" which attract a clientele from a variety of kinship units. Rather, the major significance of the *totemistic* components of both the sacred conceptual order itself and the actual organization of ritual performances is that the totems link directly to clans as kinship units.[22] Furthermore, the totemic references are so formed as to symbolize the integration of the social unit within the total order of the human condition, since the totem is usually an animal (though some-

[19] Talcott Parsons, "The Incest Taboo in Relation to Social Structure and the Socialization of the Child," in *Social Structure and Personality, op. cit.* Levi-Strauss, *Les Structures . . . , op. cit;* also see Chap. XV in Levi-Strauss' *Structural Anthropology* (New York: Basic Books, 1963).

[20] Cf. Warner, *op. cit.*, Chap. V.

[21] Durkheim, *op. cit.*

[22] *Ibid;* Levi-Strauss, *Totemism, op. cit., passim.*

times a plant) species, and thus sub-human, as well as supra-human by virtue of being a sacred entity.[23]

Besides the totems, there is a set of sacred beings which are significant at the tribal level. These figure particularly in the origin myths that explain who the people are, how they came to be what they are, and so on. Again, these are very directly integrated with the social structure. It is significant, however, that Wollunqua, in one aspect, symbolizes the corporate body of adult males who constitute the tribe, so far as this exists, not just a clan.[24] The Wawilak sisters, then, seem to symbolize, among other things, both the boys, who are absorbed into this corporate group through initiation, and the women, who are not initiated and remain permanently outside it. The story that Wollunqua "swallows" the sisters seems to involve *both* these symbolizations. Wollunqua is also very closely related to certain conditions of the physical environment, especially the seasonal cycle which is particularly dramatic in contrasting rainy and dry seasons in that part of Australia.

The incest theme is also prominent in the Wollunqua-Wawilak myth. The mythical founders are thought to have actually committed incest—indeed living men are all, sufficiently far back, the product of incestuous unions. However, the *differentiation* of human society into organized kinship units precluded the continuation of this practice, in both myth and actuality.

The religious ceremonials constitute a direct, dramatic "acting out" of the mythical beliefs in narrative form.[25] In Murngin tribal initiation ceremonies, the adult men, as a corporate group, actually play the part of the serpent Wollunqua, ceremonially "swallowing" the initiates—i.e., admitting them to membership. As Bellah, following Stanner, emphasizes, the adult man directly *participates in* the world of the sacred by dramatically playing the part of a sacred being. He actually *becomes* part of the totem or Wollunqua, as the case may be. This does not mean, as some critics of Durkheim have inferred, that the sacred beings are "reduced" to the status of secular social units, clan, or tribe. Rather, it means that the statuses of sacred object and "secular" social unit have not been differentiated.[26]

We have suggested that a primitive institutional system must successfully consolidate all the organizational elements of a society at the cultural-symbolic level. Ritual generally includes a controlled permissiveness (indeed, more than that, prescription) regarding behavior, beliefs, emotions, and so on, which are more "primitive" (or "regressive" psychologically) than those symbolically con-

[23] Later, we will see, especially in Egypt, that the religious use of animal symbolism is not confined to primitive societies, but extends well into the intermediate category. We may re-emphasize here that it is the diffuseness of the references in the sacred order, and their structural correspondence to the social order, not the totemism *per se*, that seems to be the universal among "very primitive" societies. Cf. Levi-Strauss, *Totemism*, *op. cit.* and *Structural Anthropology*, *op. cit*; also Leach, *Rethinking Anthropology*, op. cit.

[24] Warner, *op. cit.*, Chap. IX, discusses the myth of Yurlunggur or Wollunqua and the Wawilak sisters, the central myth in many Australian systems of constitutive symbolism.

[25] Cf. W. E. H. Stanner, *On Aboriginal Religion* (Melbourne: Oceania Monographs #11, 1964).

[26] This proposition applies to the sacred object as a cultural object in the sense of Chap. 2. The object is not itself "ultimate reality" but a "representation" of it, a term which Durkheim himself used.

trolled by the ritual. The Australian case offers two striking examples. Participating in ritual, men *behave* as sub-human animals; they "take the role" of the totem species or the tribal serpent. Also, it is prescribed that they ceremonially do what is otherwise strictly forbidden—namely, have sexual relations with members of categories of kin with whom marriage and sexual intercourse are otherwise forbidden as incestuous. However, this "permissiveness," far from leading to reversion to pre-cultural levels, serves as a mechanism for reinforcing commitments to maintain the cultural patterns.

Magic may also be analyzed in this context. Religious beliefs and ritual practices are integrated with the social structure through common commitments (in the form of prescribed relational patterns) to either the largest significant collectivity or its segmental units—e.g., the clans. They promote the type of societal integration that Durkheim called mechanical solidarity. Magic is the ritualization of interests and activities which cannot be fitted into this framework, which are individualized in Durkheim's sense.[27]

This is most evident in regard to the more strictly utilitarian problems of technology. In hunting, finding food, and (for peoples having settled agriculture) gardening, magic is a supplementary technique that ensures success.[28] It mobilizes supernatural forces from the realm of the sacred in favor of particular objectives but without mobilizing the collective solidarity of the community or its major units in the sense that religious ritual does. From such technological contexts, magic extends into areas such as health which more definitely involve integrative concerns. Illness is, from one point of view, the lapse of the sick person from his status as a fully integrated member of the relevant collectivities. Magical means may then help restore him to full functioning, and are very common throughout the primitive world. Black magic is the obverse; it is the primary primitive means, other than physical force, for exerting upon individuals the sanctions of negative prevention of, and punishment or exclusion for, deviant action.

Although magic's involvement with warfare and other forms of violence is complex, it fits within the same general paradigm. As Warner shows, warfare among clans is the most serious threat to the integration of Murngin society. When directed against presumptive enemies, warfare magic reinforces the internal solidarity of the warring group in order to promote its success, but does not involve a set of ritual obligations held in common with the enemies. Internally (say at the clan level), it may be effective both in promoting the clan interest and in minimizing the intervention of higher-order collectivities in the clan.[29] Such cases of magic fit the general framework of mechanisms furthering organic solidarity in Durkheim's sense.

I have suggested that the functioning of any society, perhaps particularly a primitive one, requires the institutionalization of common normative codes, which contain rules for ordering the communicative aspects of social activities. In a society like the Murngin, the societal code system may be a less obviously salient structure than kinship, religion, or technology—yet it is the cement that binds them all together.

[27] Durkheim, *The Division of Labor in Society, op. cit.*

[28] Cf. Bronislaw Malinowski, *Magic, Science and Religion* (Glencoe, Ill.: The Free Press. 1948); and *Coral Gardens and Their Magic* (New York: American, 1935).

[29] Warner, *op. cit.*

It seems that prescriptiveness [30] is the major characteristic of the Australian normative codes, it being evident that this is a highly undifferentiated type of code. Australian societies have a proliferation of kinship groupings, but these operate upon the individual's status-ascription so diffusely that he has practically a minimum of fundamental choices. Although individuals engage in a very wide variety of concrete acts—e.g., technological work, religious and magical ritual activities, recreation, and so on—they do not perform these different classes of acts *in differentiated roles* in the sense true of individuals in more developed societies. As Stanner [31] succinctly put it, life in such a society is "a one-possibility thing" for the individual.

One corollary of this statement is that the relations among the various categories of acts which individuals perform are prescribed in terms of an undifferentiated intra-societal code. For example, all rules for hunting apply to the major elements of status in the society, expecially sex, generational age, and kinship status. Once a kill is made, the normative order prescribes the way in which it should be distributed with reference to the same elements of status. Again the same elements enter fundamentally into the prescription of the ritual uses to be made of the hunt's proceeds, the persons to participate in the ritual activities, and the ways in which they will participate.

These facts constitute the core of the phenomenon we have called the undifferentiatedness of Australian society. Clearly, it embodies elementary differentiation of function by sex and age. For example, by virtue of the latter, elders have more authority than their juniors, and there is a sharp status distinction between uninitiated boys and initiated men. These bases of differentiation enter, above all, into the composition of the nuclear family, into its functions, economic and technological as well as socializing, and into the changes in family memberships at different stages of the life cycle. Beyond this, however, the society consists overwhelmingly of *segments* which are both distinguished from one another and bound together by the prescriptive rules and the practices they regulate, especially those pertaining to marriage alliances. The normative order is evidently couched at a very low level of generalization, though one clearly compatible with the maintenance of cultural control over the relevant action processes. Value patterns evidently have to legitimize a role structure differentiated only by age and sex and by loyalties to four orders of collectivity—namely, nuclear family, lineage, clan, and the rather vaguely defined tribe. With the crucial exception of "in-marrying" spouses, these membership loyalties are "concentric," with the innermost implying the others, much as residence in American society implies belonging in a local community, a state, and the federal Union. The status of in-marrying persons is the major point of possibility for role-conflict,[32] and is hence the most likely point for developmental change to take hold. Despite the rigidity of the prescriptive system, a close look at this type of society reveals many possible sources of instability and structural change.

[30] This use of the term "prescription" is an effort to build upon and generalize from Needham's and other anthropologists' usage. See Needham, *Structure and Sentiment*, *op. cit.*

[31] W. E. H. Stanner, "The Dreaming," in William Lessa and Evon Z. Vogt (eds.), *Reader in Comparative Religion* (Evanston: Row, Peterson, 1958).

[32] Warner, *op. cit.*, Chap. VI.

The Transition to the "Advanced" Primitive Type [33]

In the Australian societies, the core structure of the societal community as a whole is the affinal system regulated by the prescriptive marriage rules. As noted, this complex of norms binds the segmentary lineages and clans together into a society, though not a sharply bounded one. We would expect structural change to become evident at this point, whatever its causes.

A most important source of change arises when the strict status equivalence of the intermarrying kinship groups breaks down. A given group may then attempt to improve its status or its position for controlling resources by exercising preferences in giving or receiving spouses through establishing special relations with particular subgroups *within* the categories of prescribed affinal groups. That is, marriage alliances come to be made with a view to the advantages which the affinal groups may be able to bestow upon one another, and hence involve an element of bargaining that cannot arise in purely prescriptive systems. Here, the potential for evolutionary advance depends upon the degree to which generalized grounds of status differentiation are institutionalized and enabled to influence the preferences.

For evolutionary changes to emerge, these developments must be complemented by a generalization in the solidarity of the clan, so that common identities prevent the more advantaged lineages from asserting themselves as independent clans. Then a lineage in one clan may develop a special solidarity with a particular lineage in the prescribed alliance clan, and effectively exercise systematic preferences for that lineage in choosing its spouses. In such transitional systems, the pattern of the "circulation" of spouses and of the alliance solidarities is the result of *both* prescriptive cycling and preferential subcycling.[34] However, the long run evolutionary tendency is clearly toward the attenuation and elimination of the developmentally restrictive prescriptive regulations, which inherently favor the generalized equality of categorical collaterals.

Under certain conditions, strong economic pressures may support this tendency. Australian conditions narrowly limit the manageable size of a band, and the band must enjoy a certain autonomy from others in the clan. Settled residence, conditioned by agriculture and/or the use of domestic animals, tends to increase these pressures. Instead of rather vague rights to hunting and gathering in a large territory, specific kinship groups may come to hold more

[33] Because of our severe limitations of space, the following section cannot attempt to follow through the stages and processes of transition it surveys in terms of specific illustrative examples. Therefore, it is more in the nature of an "ideal type" construction than either the preceding section on Australian aboriginal society or the final section on the "advanced" primitive societies. Its purpose is merely to fill the gap of continuity in a minimum of space, so as to make the connection between the two broad stage-types comprehensible. It does not present a comprehensive analysis of any of the large number of societies that seem to fall within this gap.

[34] Needham, *op. cit.;* Leach, *op. cit.;* also *The Political Systems of Highland Burma* (Boston: Beacon Paperbacks, 1964); Jack Goody (ed.), *Developmental Cycles of Domestic Groups* (Cambridge: Cambridge Papers in Social Anthropology, 1958), especially Leach's chapter, "Concerning Trobriand Clans and the Kinship Category Tabu."

clear-cut *property* rights, often to the *exclusive* use of land tracts for cultivation and/or pasturing. The attendant economic advances may cause an increase in population, thus enhancing the pressure to lineage-segmentation. Furthermore, advances in economic organization and the crystallization of property rights increase the lineage's stake in effective control of territory, and hence in the clarity and stability of community and societal boundaries.[35]

If residence and utilization of land is to be stable, the predominant emphasis in defining the community must shift from the affinal aspect of kinship to independent territorial factors. Then, to a new degree the societal community *must* become endogamous in its *external* relations. Internally, however, it is problematic whether lineage segmentation will lead to status *differentiation* among lineages, rather than to the mere multiplication of structurally identical units.

Some occupational specialization tends to emerge with these developments, although it does not become a primary basis of social differentiation until much later in societal evolution. Within sharp limits, however, certain lineages may differentiate themselves from others by undertaking specialized functions or controlling special resources. The most important of these seem to involve trade, especially vis-à-vis the outside; warfare; and special religious functions, such as the custodianship of sacred places.[36]

On the whole, however, the main line of growth for the most primitive type of society involves not (or not only) such particular specializations, but the differentiation of lineages on a generalized axis of prestige, advantage, and responsibility. If this is the case, two questions arise: Why is the lineage the crucial unit? What are the bases of differentiation?

On the first question, the very small kinship units—e.g., nuclear family, joint family, cognatic household, and so on, are evidently too small and deeply embedded in the articulations between the obligations of descent and affinity. Above all, it is most unlikely that their members can sufficiently control their marriages—i.e., heads of the lineage or village, not just the parents, control the marriages of children; institutionalized control by the children themselves evolves only *much* later. The clan, on the other hand, is too deeply grounded in the prescriptive elements of the marriage system. Moreover, the very bases of institutionalizing status differentials tend to make it too traditionalized, amorphous, and non-corporate to become an *agency* in a broad social movement.

It seems that in most cases some variant of the lineage type of organization, having become the most important intermediate size unit, serves as the society's *primary* agent of differentiation. It is strong enough to control the smaller kin units and to assure them sufficiently favorable marriage terms, unless it is on the downgrade itself. Also, it is not the main responsible guarantor of the traditional system.

Two primary sets of forces seem to support the emergence of differentiation among lineages. One—very familiar in our traditions of social thought—is the tendency to differential advantage, property in land being its most important vehicle. Positions which are advantageous, whether by virtue of pro-

[35] Cf. Meyer Fortes and E. E. Evans-Pritchard (eds.), *African Political Systems* (Oxford: Oxford University Press, 1940); I. Schapera, *Government and Politics in Tribal Societies* (London: Watts, 1956).

[36] Raymond Firth, *Primitive Polynesian Economy* (London: Routledge, 1939).

ductivity, centrality of location, or other factors, tend to be systematically preempted. Especially during periods of segmentation and population growth, the less advantaged lineages tend to be forced into inferior locations and to be deprived of resources. Despite the variety of bases of such advantage, it is certainly difficult to maintain the strict egalitarianism presupposed by any system of the equivalence of clan collaterals, once there are firm institutions of property.

The other basis arises from the growth in importance of the *societal* collectivity as such, including its tendency to become more definitely bounded. In turn, this must involve the increased importance of its distinctive religious grounds of legitimation, of its territorial controls over its resource base, and of the common identity of its population. Hence, there is pressure to *symbolize* the collective identity of the society more definitely and explicitly and also to develop more effective instrumentalities for its functioning as a system, especially in the contexts we consider governmental.

These two reference points of development concern the structure of action systems at the most general level, as discussed in the preceding chapter. The importance of land and the territorial ordering of society, both in terms of external boundaries and internal land distributions, is rooted in the importance of the physical world among the factors *conditioning* social action. Society-wide prestige, and its relation to political leadership and the assumption of collective responsibilities, basically concerns the importance of having leverage to *control* the conditioning factors. Furthermore, no such ramified process of societal differentiation can conceivably consolidate itself unless the upper groups acquire more generalized religious legitimation from the constitutive symbol system of the society, as well as the instrumentalities of power as such.[37]

It does not seem crucial to assign priority to one or the other of the above sets of factors. If different groups press their own particular interests too far and too fast and neglect the development of integrating factors, particularly religious legitimation, the society will generally break up, the relatively nonfavored elements seceding to form independent societies. If cultural or political centralization advances too far and if adequate bases of kinship and of economic-political membership units are not developed, it is unlikely that the new level of cultural and political organization can be maintained.

Thus, the most likely evolutionary development is a *stratified* society. There are degrees of stratification, but to emerge significantly, a stratified society must break radically with the egalitarianism of a strictly prescriptive affinal system based upon the strict equivalence of all same-category collaterals. Lineage units will tend to exchange spouses on a basis of *advantage*, high-prestige units allying themselves with other high-prestige units.[38] The high-prestige units, then, become the focus of new elements of solidarity within the societal collectivity, elements which are likely to be at once political and

[37] There is a type of case which might seem to be an exception to this statement: namely, that in which a group subordinates another group by military conquest. This is not differentiation in the present sense. It has played an important part in processes of social change, but usually the conquerors are a foreign group, not a structural segment of the original society. Furthermore, it is a rare, limiting case when such a group altogether eschews claim to religious legitimation and operates in terms of its naked self-interest alone.

[38] Charles D. Ackerman, "Three Studies of Affinal Collectivity" (Ph.D. Thesis, Harvard University, 1965); Leach, *Political Systems of Highland Burma, op. cit.*

religious, with empirically varying emphases as between these two components. These developments tend to become embedded in the kinship structure itself, involving the hierarchical principles that often inhere in lineage organization—e.g., seniority on the basis of generation status. The emergence of stratification, then, tends to culminate in the elevation of a single lineage to privileged rank, and perhaps of its senior member to a top authority and prestige position. That is, there exists a very general tendency toward the emergence of monarchy having both political and religious foundations.

The basis of community must become radically redefined to include the patterns of "class" and preferential marriage. The societal community comes to be conceived as an ethnic-territorial group. If descent is traced back far enough, all of its members are believed to be descended from common ancestors. But this comprehensive descent-community is *not* backed by systematic intermarriage patterns that pervade the whole society. Common descent is likely to be associated with common culture in various ways—e.g., language, but especially religion. Furthermore, the emergence of differentiated political authority places a strong premium on the territorial aspects of community solidarity. In short, the societal collectivity becomes a *tribe*, an ethnic group maintaining jurisdiction over a territorial area.

Once this transition has taken place, it becomes less and less possible to maintain the more primitive coincidence between kinship status and residential location. The general shift from prescription to preference is associated with various increases in mobility and opportunities for dominance-dependency relations. Hence, the territorial sub-units of the society, from broad regions down to villages, tend to shift from uniformity toward pluralism and diversity. This is greatly accentuated as stratification evolves to the point of monarchy, which generally involves a central seat of authority and prestige. Inevitably, very diverse elements are attracted to such a seat, either permanently or temporarily. Moreover, the principles for selecting the population of such a capital can hardly be confined to kinship terms.

An ethnic-territorial societal community clearly requires a new, more generalized basis of legitimation, both for its authority system and for the identity of the community itself. It is no longer a "seamless web" of kinship relations in which the primary units (e.g., clans) in principle are equivalent to one another. It is a system which has become *differentiated*, first by the varying statuses of its lineage units, and then between kinship and non-kinship (e.g., region of residence) bases of status. This requires the institutionalization of more generalized constitutive definitions of who "we" are and of the natures of the diverse units included in the "we-ness." Above all, kinship and locality units are generally independently variable, and a prestige scale involving and interrelating both must be institutionalized—e.g., the "lower-class resident" of the capital community still enjoys a certain prestige as compared with the "higher-class provincial." [39]

Furthermore, the religious tradition is generally differentiated into elements which are associated with the societal leadership institutionalized in the upper groups (particularly the royal lineage) and elements which are particular to the local, parochial communities and kinship groups. Thus, the class dimen-

[39] S. F. Nadel, A *Black Byzantium* (Oxford: Oxford University Press, 1951).

sion which we have sketched involves, very fundamentally, differential access to the *higher* elements of a new, more differentiated sacred order.[40]

In the most primitive societies, as we have mentioned, the societal community is based overwhelmingly on affinal solidarities. The general processes of differentiation just sketched introduce a second axis into the community structure—which can be controlled only by more complex integrative mechanisms. Territoriality both bounds the community externally and grounds the institution of property in relation to territorial location (i.e., property in land) internally. Residential location and control of economic resources, then, become *independent* of kinship; the operative unit—a lineage at some level—has *two* independent main bases for its position in the system, kinship and property.

In very primitive systems, the most generalized and significant exchange transactions are exchanges of spouses, directly or indirectly, in a circuit. As a consequence of differentiation, spouses come to be exchangeable for prestige and/or property advantage and vice-versa. Position in the system of stratification, as sketched above, is the *resultant* of the interplay of two media of circulating valuables.

In understanding this interplay, we must understand that a marriage is a large, relatively infrequent unit of commitment for a relatively small kinship group; to "give" a daughter or son to another group is a major "expenditure" of mobile resources. Similarly, the transfer of proprietorship in land-holdings is a major transaction that can occur but seldom. What a marriage generally does, then, is commit the wife-giving and wife-receiving units to continuing exchanges of valuable objects, starting possibly with a "bride-price." These are usually balanced to compensate the wife- or husband-giving groups for its resource expenditure, although status differentials frequently complicate the exchange relations.

Property, at this level of evolution, is *not* a differentiated, strictly economic category, but involves components of diffuse influence or prestige and political authority or power, as well as control of economic resources. In some cases, the territorial involvements of landed property may make lineages practically into petty sovereignties within the larger tribal community. Thus, the reason lineage is like a state within a federal nation, but is integrated into the larger system by much more informal mechanisms, particularly the interchanges of spouses and the benefits of its diffuse property statuses.

The components of the property complex are institutionally bound together in much the same way as the components of the most primitive institutional codes that we have discussed. However, it does permit considerable variability in concrete action, even besides that deriving from the basic independence between the complexes of affinal and property relationships. As we will see, the types of more advanced primitive societies differ with the relative weight of the independent components of the property complex, the religio-cultural, the political, and the economic, as well as with the degree of differentiation between the affinal-kinship and property complexes. Hence, there is no neatly uniform, universal type.

In the most strikingly stratified cases, however, the royal lineages, which may become both very large and very compactly organized through the practice of polygyny, tend to acquire very tight control of the more mobile economic

[40] Daryll Forde (ed.), *African Worlds* (Oxford: Oxford University Press, 1954).

and political resources throughout the society, largely by arranging politically shrewd marriage alliances that heavily obligate their affines. This seems to be an indispensable condition of such a royal lineage's capacity to discharge its responsibilities on behalf of the tribe as a whole. These responsibilities may include religious rituals, relatively secular ceremonials enhancing societal solidarity, the management of the political "bureaucracy" and the military organization, and the like. Stratification, then, is the institution which makes possible a great increase in the relative centralization of societal responsibility and, with it, collective effectiveness. At this evolutionary level, high status does not rest mainly on superior control of political power or economic resources. It makes possible the institutionalized concentration of such control which underlies such superiority itself.

Ultimately, perhaps two bases of prestige are especially crucial to the capacities of highly superior royal lineages to exploit their positions in the community, particularly its kinship structuring. First is the central role of the royal lineage in the more generalized religious system, a system which can legitimize a much more differentiated and larger-scale society. Second is the freeing of resources from the very tight ascription to kinship characteristic of the most primitive societies. The emergence of property in land as a structurally independent element greatly enhances resource mobility.

This mobility requires the establishment of equivalences in the input-output interchanges between lineage units—e.g., as regards the relative values of marital alliances and proprietary controls. It is prestige level in the stratification system that signifies the "price" at which such components can be interchanged. Institutional mechanisms for the flexible determination of this prestige element comprise a basic requisite of the advanced type of primitive society.

Types of Advanced Primitive Societies

To conclude this chapter, we may briefly consider a particularly important aspect of the variation among the more advanced primitive societies. The most favorable "field" seems to be the African kingdoms, which present both a wide variety and have been the most thoroughly studied, mainly by British anthropologists.[41]

Unlike the Australian type, all advanced primitive societies are characterized by stratification and by some kind of central political organization based upon relatively secure territorial boundaries. Furthermore, the political element always involves a fusion of what we consider political and religious components, which are never clearly differentiated at this stage of evolution. There can exist, however, different relative emphases between the religious and political aspects, and this seems to comprise the most important axis of variation, at least for our purposes.

A very clear-cut example of a people who have developed a monarchical institution with a paramount religious emphasis is the Shilluk of the upper-Nile

[41] Most comprehensively reported, apart from the many monographs, in *African Political Systems*, edited by Fortes and Evans-Pritchard, *op. cit.*, and in Schapera, *op. cit.* I have also relied particularly upon Evans-Pritchard's account of the Shilluk in his *Essays in Social Anthropology* (London: Faber and Faber, 1962); and on Nadel's account of the Nupe in his *Black Byzantium, op. cit.*

Sudan. Clearly established among the Shilluk is a divine kingship that is especially interesting because of its resemblance to the ancient Egyptian system and the Sudan's proximity to Egypt.

The Shilluk society is highly segmented, which is perhaps attributable to the fact that it is strung out along the east bank of the Nile.[42] There is also a sharp institutional division between the northern and southern sectors of the society. Significantly, the capital and seat of the monarchy, Fashoda, is situated on the line between north and south, and the chiefs of the two sections function very importantly in the selection of new kings.

The Shilluk upper class consists of descendants of former kings. By a variety of arrangements, their residences are dispersed throughout the territory, not concentrated in or near the capital. In part, this is a consequence of the matrilineal kinship system, but there is also a specific rule that princes (i.e., sons of a king's wife) should be brought up in the mother's natal community and never in the capital. The local chieftains reside side by side with the parochial lineage groups, a status shared by clans of royal "retainers." They are not generally members of the royal lineage, but are the heads of the local lineages. Moreover, they are nominated for their positions by their own lineages, not by royal appointment, though some kind of royal consent is customary. They do not constitute an administrative apparatus of the central "government."

The royal institution is structured about the divinity of the king.[43] The current king is not only the heir, but actually the incarnation of the divine mythical founder, Nyikang, who is the basis of the legitimacy and identity of the Shilluk as a people. When a king dies, Nyikang becomes incarnated in an effigy kept in his principal provincial shrine in the northern sector. About a year later, the effigy is ceremonially reincarnated in the king-elect, who is not only legitimized by Nyikang, but *becomes* Nyikang. The ritual procedures of the investiture clearly stress not only the divinity of the king, but also his function in integrating the principal components of the society. He is nominated by the two chiefs of the northern and southern sectors, who *must* concur. Then representatives of all the main structural segments must ritually assent to the nomination.

Shilluk religion represents a further generalization and systematization of the more primitive type of sacred or ritual order. The function of bearing and implementing the sacred traditions is centered in the royal lineage and upper class, particularly the institution of kingship.

Among the Shilluk, the integrative aspects of kingship have emerged without a very marked development of the more administrative and politically activistic aspects. They are settled, and do have a considerably higher-order economy than the Australians. Yet, for example, they conduct warfare by mobilizing their essentially independent lineage units, not by virtue of the king's invoking standing military obligations that cross-cut the lineage structure and are at his disposal.

[42] The neighboring Dinka and Nuer are rather similarly segmented, but lack a monarchical institution and are thus rather less advanced in our terms. Cf. E. E. Evans-Pritchard, *The Nuer* (Oxford: Clarendon Press, 1940).

[43] See Godfrey Lienhardt, "The Shilluk of The Upper Nile," in Forde (ed.), *African Worlds, op. cit.*, as well as the Evans-Pritchard essay noted above.

These structures may well constitute an early stage in the development of a type of society which in later chapters will appear to be very significant in subsequent societal evolution. This important type rests on the integration of larger solidary structures through the association of basically equal sub-components. Only after much further evolution can such components be individuals; in the earlier stages, they are always kinship groups, generally lineages. The Shilluk divine kingship evidently provides a sacred umbrella under which the segmental units can be consolidated into an associative structure, their divisive tendencies checked, and a positive solidarity developed. In a pattern similar to the Shilluk confederation of tribal units, ancient lineages associated to form more advanced societal structures of the small-scale *polis* type throughout the eastern Mediterranean and Mesopotamian regions.

The second principal type of advanced primitive societies is represented by a number of examples, varying considerably, described in the *African Political Systems* symposium. In this type, the political component of the functionally diffuse leadership institutions hold a certain primacy over the religious component. The monarchical institutions are critically important to the differentiation of the upper class and strongly institutionalize a rather general and diffuse precedence of societal solidarity over the interests of segmental units.

A principal characteristic of this societal type is the development of a royal administrative apparatus which, in varying ways and degrees, can be considered a government—which exists only in the most rudimentary sense among the Shilluk. Fortes and Evans-Pritchard [44] strongly emphasize the importance of *centralized* command of force in bringing this about. A major factor here is the development of a centralized military apparatus for conducting wars against outside societies, with the line between defense and aggressive conquest or raiding being rather indefinite, as it frequently is in the history of warfare. Perhaps as important, however, is the use of the military to maintain internal order, especially to counteract the tendencies toward dissolution and rebellion which are endemic in these societies. Significantly, *all* of them have histories of continual violence and disorder, including frequent contests for the kingship among different branches of the royal line and different segmental groups. Perhaps the Zulu kingdom at its height was the most extreme example of the tendency to militarization within societies of this type.[45]

However important the military factor, and however great the possibilities for tyranny, these aspects never comprised the whole story. The religious status of the monarchical institution and the authority system has generally been as crucial in this type as in the first. The uses of authority by the king and upper groups must be understood to represent the collective interest of the tribe, as legitimized in the religious tradition. Compared to other primitive societal types, the religious tradition has usually been developed to a much higher level of generality, particularly with respect to the divinities which concern the tribe as a whole, the greatly accentuated theme of the descent of the

[44] Fortes and Evans-Pritchard (eds.), "Introduction" to *African Political Systems, op. cit.*

[45] Cf. Max Gluckman, "The Kingdom of the Zulu of South Africa," in Fortes and Evans-Pritchard (eds.), *op. cit.*

entire tribe from ancestors of an heroic past, and the conception of the founder-king as the fountainhead of socio-cosmic order and benefits.[46] Africa has been an area of pronounced mobility, and many contemporary kingdoms were founded sufficiently recently so that the successions of monarchs from the founders to the present rulers is traced circumstantially and maintained as tradition. That is, these societies have somewhat of a history, in a sense not true for the primitive Australian.

A critical characteristic of this type of society is the development of civil administrative systems more or less clearly differentiated from both the military and the more strictly religious organizations. The connection between the central "administration" and the chieftainships of regional and local lineage groups is a crucial structural problem in these societies. Unlike the Shilluk, there is a general tendency for local administrators to be appointed by the central authority. Moreover, they tend to develop powers of taxation, administration of justice, and the like, which are only very partially (often not at all, in formal terms) controlled by the local groups. Particularly important, as Fortes and Evans-Pritchard point out, is that the central authorities of all these societies develop systematic institutions for regulating the administration of justice—i.e., for ensuring that cases are treated in accordance with the accepted norms of the *central* tradition.[47]

Both military and civil "bureaucracies" of these types are clearly points from which institutions can become increasingly differentiated from the kinship nexus. However, the political, as distinguished from the religious, focus tends to impart a relatively strict hierarchism. This generally inhibits the development both of associational solidarities that are independent of "line" authority and of unit autonomy that is more strictly economic than political.

A particularly clear case of modest development toward the more "political" advanced primitive type is the Bemba tribe described by Audrey Richards.[48] The Nupe, as thoroughly portrayed by Nadel,[49] approach, under Islamic influence, the borderline between a primitive society and an archiac one. It approaches what Weber called a "patrimonial" monarchy, having a very extensive administrative bureaucracy, organized handicrafts, controlled trade, and even the beginnings of a monetary system.

[46] Several chapters in Forde (ed.), *op. cit.*, are quite clear in these connections, perhaps especially "The Fon of Dahomey" by P. Mercier.

[47] *Cf.* Schapera, *op. cit.*

[48] Audrey Richards, "The Political System of the Bemba Tribe—North-Eastern Rhodesia," in Fortes and Evans-Pritchard (eds.), *op. cit.*

[49] Nadel, *A Black Byzantium*, *op. cit.*

four

archaic societies

We will now discuss the second of the three main stages of societal evolution, the "intermediate" stage, characterized by the development of *written* language.

There are cases, as we have mentioned, in which predominantly primitive societies interpenetrate with literate cultures, one such instance being the Nupe since their conquest by the Islamic Fullani. The Nupe are, however, clearly peripheral to an essentially foreign religio-cultural complex, whereas in a fully intermediate society, an indigenous literate tradition is constitutive of the culture.

We shall distinguish two *principal* substages of intermediate society, the archaic and the "advanced intermediate". By archaic, we mean the first major stage in the evolution of intermediate society, that of craft literacy and cosmological religion. The advanced stage is characterized by full upper-class literacy and, on the cultural side, by what Bellah [1] calls an *historic* religion, one which has broken through to *philosophical* levels of generalization and systematization. Such religions develop for the first time conceptions of a *supernatural* order in Durkheim's full sense, one sharply differentiated from any "order of nature."

An archaic "cosmological" religio-cultural system generalizes and systematizes the constitutive symbolism of the society much more highly than the cultural system of any primitive society. This cultural elaboration is linked with the literacy of priesthoods and their capacity to maintain a stable written tradition. The literacy is, however, still esoteric and limited to specialized groups

[1] Robert N. Bellah, "Religious Evolution," *The American Sociological Review* (June, 1964).

—hence, it is craft literacy. Besides the religio-magical, its most important specialized use is for administrative purposes. Only in advanced intermediate societies is literacy centering about the mastery of a central literary tradition a characteristic of all upper-class adult males—e.g., the upper-caste Hindus or the Chinese gentry.

A cosmological cultural system is generally interpreted for, and ritually mediated to, the society as a whole by specialized temple priesthoods. The priesthoods administer *cults*, the functioning and ritual benefits of which are no longer so rigidly ascribed to underlying kinship and local community structures as in even advanced primitive societies. In certain instances, the temple itself may become a focal unit of the social organization—e.g., in economic connections. In general, the function of cultural legitimation has become differentiated, generalized, and though closely bound to the highest echelon of the society (e.g., the king), entrusted to the priestly groups.[2]

On the "political" side, in the sense of the term used in the last chapter, there has been a parallel differentiation. *All* archaic societies have an administrative apparatus elaborated well beyond the level of such societies as the Shilluk or Bemba. Both priestly and administrative functions are generally controlled by lineages rather than appointed individuals, particular statuses typically being hereditary. Moreover, the political and religious offices often overlap very significantly. They are, however, sufficiently distinct so that we can regard religious and secular stratification as being considerably differentiated. Yet, each tends to crystallize about a three-class pattern: the very top, asociated with the charisma of the monarch and the exercise of his combined religious and political authority; a less centralized middle group responsible for the more routine functioning of the society; and the mass of the common people, who are, above all, tillers of the soil. The last also includes craftsmen and even merchants, who become increasingly prominent with further development, particularly as functionaries of the great households or temples standing in client-like relations with the leading proprietary lineages.[3]

This further differentiation seems to account for a shift away from the pattern prescribed by the two major types of advanced primitive society we touched on at the end of Chapter 3. The two cases of archaic society which we will discuss in the present chapter, ancient Egypt and Mesopotamia, exemplify a curious reversal compared to the Shilluk and the Bemba. Egypt had the most highly developed institution of divine kingship in the known world. At the same time, the structure of the society was not segmental in the Shilluk manner, but notably hierarchical and, in a special sense, "bureaucratic." In Mesopotamia, kingship was notably *not* fused with divinity, but the underlying base of the society was much more segmental. This segmentation, however, developed in the form of the urban communities—rather than kinship groups as such—which were the most important member units of the society. We will suggest that the very prominent development of the intermediate level in the societal structures

[2] Cf. Talcott Parsons, "Evolutionary Universals in Society," *The American Sociological Review* (June, 1964).

[3] As archaeologists have long emphasized, these developments generally also involve very significant developments in urbanization, in some sense. The comparative evidence on this point is well summarized in *Courses Toward Urban Life,* edited by Robert J. Braidwood and Gordon Willey (Chicago: Aldine Publishing Company, 1962).

impelled this difference. Given the cosmological level of cultural symbolization, the control of such a complex society (compared, for example, to the Shilluk) required a tightly controlled apparatus of both ritualization and political administration. In the case of Mesopotamia, however, the relative decentralization of the religious system permitted the constituent structural units much greater autonomy. But it is significant that the political apex of Mesopotamian society was not nearly so stable as that of Egypt.

Archaic societies have emerged independently in many parts of the world, most importantly in the Indian subcontinent, China, Southeast Asia, and the New World (the Aztecs, Mayans, and Incas). We have chosen to examine Egypt and Mesopotamia, however, because they have been so thoroughly investigated by archaeologists and because of their historic connections with more advanced societies we will discuss subsequently.

Our treatment of advanced intermediate societies will be organized in two chapters, the distinctions between which are somewhat complicated, but not arbitrary. Chapter 5 will deal with a spectrum of cases which achieved high organizational levels on a considerable scale and maintained considerable continuity in their basic patternings over some centuries, but which have conspicuously failed to generate the crucial transition to the *modern* phase of social evolution upon their own resources and developmental potentialities. We view these societies very much in the perspective of Max Weber, concerning ourselves with the problem of why they did not develop the crucial combinations of modernizing factors which appeared in the modern West.

Chapter 6 will deal with two cases of a very different order—namely, Israel and Greece in certain critical periods of their development. Both were tiny societies compared with Egypt, Mesopotamia, or Persia; their political independence was inherently precarious, and both lost it after brief periods. They were not very important in the civilizational complexes of their own time, yet both produced cultural innovations of the most crucial importance for the long-run future: the religion of Jahweh and the more or less secular culture of Greece. In combination with other factors, these served to lay the foundations for the emergence of the modern societal type, and as such deserve special treatment.

Ancient Egypt

Let us start by noting that Egypt was definitely literate, but predominantly in the special sense of craft literacy. Literacy was used primarily for invoking and maintaining religio-magical formulae and for administrative accounting.[4] Literacy and a corresponding level of education seem not to have penetrated the entire upper class generally, as it did later in post-exilic Israel, Greece, Rome, Brahman India, or post-Confucian China.

Second, Egypt was rather sharply bounded, both politically and culturally, a condition fostered by the unique geographical location of the Nile Valley, isolated east and west by deserts. Two boundaries were relatively open, the Mediterranean Coast and the attenuated desert of the upper Nile.[5] The vast

[4] William F. Edgerton, "The Government and the Governed in the Egyptian Empire," *Journal of Near Eastern Studies* (July, 1947).

[5] John A. Wilson, "Egypt," in H. and A. Frankfort, John A. Wilson, and Thorkild Jacobsen (eds.), *Before Philisophy* (Baltimore: Penguin Books, 1949), p. 39ff.

distance between these open boundaries, one bordering on Lower Egypt and the other on Upper Egypt, was probably very important. Egypt's highly distinctive system, at once religious and political, was closer culturally to its more "primitive" neighbors in the upper Nile region than any others.[6] The Hebrews' sense of Egyptian culture's foreigness indicates how sharp were the differences at the Mediterranean boundaries.

Third, Egypt certainly had a clearly marked system of stratification that included the lower classes. Here it is significant that conquest evidently played a secondary role in Egyptian history. However "authoritarian" Egyptian rule may seem from modern viewpoints, there is little question that all classes authentically belonged to the same society. Though considerably differentiated, Egyptian society attained a unique pattern of centralized integration which, except for a few periods of disorganization, remained intact for a very long time.[7]

The most distinctive feature of Egyptian society was the institution of kingship, a complex associated with many other components. Among the known institutions of monarchy, perhaps it accentuates most not the divinization of the king, but his actual *divinity*. It was inherent in the Egyptian conception that to be the king *was* to be divine.[8] The two categories were inseparable—no human or ritual agency made the king divine, though of course he was concurrently regarded as human. The kingship was a primary aspect of the sacred order itself, and of its functioning to regulate the cosmic order of both human affairs and of organic and inorganic nature.[9] Quite unlike the Greek or even the Mesopotamian gods, the Egyptian gods did not *intervene* in human affairs, did not "rule" them or manipulate the political leaders of human societies. The ruling of human affairs was integral to the divine order itself.[10]

This does not mean that the Egyptians considered the human *condition* itself divine, but exactly the contrary. Compared to the primitive situation, the gap between divine and human was vast. *Only* through the divinity of kingship and its intimate associations could human beings relate themselves to the divine. Ordinary people could not *participate in* the sacred order, they could only be articulated with it.

This articulation was accomplished mainly by an immensely ramified cult system which spread throughout Egypt and the performances of which related to myriads of gods conceived both on particularistic, local and on general, cosmic grounds, but which was legitimized largely through the charisma of the pharaoh's divinity. The pharaoh in a certain sense delegated his charismatic powers to the whole corps of priestly officials.[11] Evidently this delegation was partly legitimized by the patent impossibility of the pharaoh's performing all the

[6] Among tribes we have mentioned, especially the Shilluk. Cf. Henri Frankfort, *Kingship and The Gods* (Chicago: The University of Chicago Press, 1948), Book I, especially Chapter 14, on this general point.

[7] William F. Edgerton, "The Question of Feudal Institutions in Ancient Egypt" in R. Coulborn (ed.), *Feudalism in History* (Princeton: Princeton University Press, 1959).

[8] Henri Frankfort: *Ancient Egyptian Religion* (New York: Harper Torchbooks, 1961), p. 43.

[9] Unlike the Shilluk kingship, no lower-order human agency was required to legitimize the succeeding pharaoh.

[10] Frankfort, *Kingship and the Gods, op. cit., passim.*

[11] Wilson, *op. cit.*, pp. 96–101.

cult functions himself. The highest functionaries of this religious regime constituted a major element of the upper class, but others occupied positions at a variety of lower levels. The pharaoh's divinity was thus the basis of the ramified system of temple priesthoods which not only held responsibility for the cults but also administered immense economic resources and interpenetrated with the political organization of the society.[12]

The primary, though not exclusive, principles of organization were probably linked both to kinship and to property in land. Certainly closeness of kinship with the royal lineage was a primary criterion of status. Polygyny and large harems, maintained by the king, the members of his lineage, and other high nobles, provided a large pool of persons who were qualified by hereditary status for high preferment—it has been estimated that it was not unusual for a pharaoh to have two hundred actual sons.[13] The class structure, then, may have been symbolized by the pyramid itself, with close articulation to the divine world being the primary criterion of status. Here status was diffuse, cutting across the sharper differentiation of later societies into religious and secular organizations and functions. Yet it could break through the very strict forms of kinship ascription, making it possible for able people to be advanced more routinely from lower to higher positions of service. It could, hence, be much more bureaucratized than any primitive society. Most essential among these developments was a sharpening of the hierarchical distinction between the sacred and the secular worlds. The top was *more* sacred compared to primitive systems, and the bottom *more* profane. This differentiation, however, did not yet result in the generalized dualism characterizing the historic religions of Bellah's analysis.[14] Both spheres remained within a single system of order, neither "natural" nor "supernatural" in the sense normally meant in Western culture, the basic differentiation between them having not yet emerged.[15] The archaic development seems to involve differentiation between those aspects of a socially structured action system directly related to the sacred grounds of being and those related to it only secondarily, mediated through the king and the priests of the pharaonic cult.

The "elevation" of the Pharaoh did not merely accord a special status to an individual, but created a massive institutional structure, the royal *lineage*, to head an aristocracy that was evidently rather tightly integrated. Apparently this aristocracy staffed the higher echelons of the two major institutional structures that, besides the monarchy itself, were basically new—the elaborate religious cult system with its priesthoods and the "civil" bureaucracy, both of which comprised many levels above the "common people."

In developmental perspective, the "civil" bureaucracy appears to be the most striking innovation. Observers since Herodotus have never ceased wondering at the massive construction achievements of the Egyptians—the pyramids, the temples, the palaces, and the water-control and irrigation system of the Nile

[12] John A. Wilson, *The Culture of Ancient Egypt* (Chicago: Phoenix Books, 1951), especially Chaps. VIII and X.

[13] Edgerton, *op. cit.*

[14] "Religious Evolution," *op. cit.*

[15] Here we call attention to Durkheim's justification of his refusal to use the concept "supernatural" in discussing Australian totemism: Since an order of nature in the "historic" sense has not been defined, one cannot contrast a supernatural order to it. I have not adhered to this usage, but have allowed for the validity of the point.

Valley. These feats depended on the organization of human services for collective goals on bases of legitimation that transcended kinship ties. Broadly, although the supervisory functions were exercised only by an hereditary aristocracy, status in which was fundamentally through kinship relation to, or direct appointment from, the royal lineage itself, skilled labor and massive manpower were mobilized for "public works" primarily on bases other than those of kinship or later "feudalism." [16]

Physical products, notably grain, could be mobilized in amounts great enough to permit their storage and territorial redistribution, establishing a more generalized means of support and payment for the more complex division of labor and for assurance against famine.

Among ancient Empires of comparable scope, Egypt seems to have been notably nonmilitaristic. It is unlikely that sheer assertion of superior force leaving others no alternative to submission was the main process by which a lineage established itself in a position as preeminent as that of the pharaonic institution. Probably the cultural aspects of the process were more important. However important political power in the narrower sense may have been, it must have been highly dependent on this unique system of cultural legitimation.

This development involved considerable technological innovations.[17] Civilized Egypt was always a settled agricultural economy. The degree of literacy achieved was very significant for bureaucratic administration, and techniques of stone-working, metallurgy, textile production, and so on advanced very significantly beyond earlier levels.

The crucial innovation, however, evidently pertained to manpower organization, the mobilization of human services for large collective enterprises. Its basis seems to have been the population's diffuse commitment to a "welfare" type of state, leadership of which clearly focused on the kingship.[18] It was never a modern bureaucracy, however, largely because service within it lacked the form of an occupational role. In Weber's scheme, Egyptian administration is perhaps best characterized as patrimonial, although this is only a very approximate characterization. Manpower was requisitioned on the basis of the diffuse religio-political form of commitment and obligation. Although relatively little is known about the exact conditions of service, remuneration, exemptions, and the like, the broad pattern seems relatively clear.

Even the rudiments of differentiation that we take for granted in modern systems were not yet present in the Egyptian pattern. For those whose roles primarily involved the performance of services, as distinguished from assumption of leadership responsibility, the main pattern seems to have been a response to the leadership's invoking obligations that were concomitants of the status of membership in the societal community and various of its segmental units. The closest modern analogy is the military service performed by an ordinary citizen, except that the leader of the Egyptian bureaucracy did not need a special emergency to invoke legitimate obligations. Thus there was essentially no private sphere within which the "citizen" was autonomous, and which legally obliged the "government" to negotiate with him about the terms of his service. Service performances for Egyptian public programs were not hired from a labor force in

[16] Edgerton, *op. cit.*
[17] Wilson, *The Culture of Ancient Egypt, op. cit.*, Chaps. II and III.
[18] Wilson, "Egypt," *op. cit.*, p. 90.

anything like the modern sense. Rather, people served under ascribed obligations, not feudally to particular aristocratic lineages, but communally more or less to a whole society which was most basically differentiated only between the kingship complex and the common people. It was a kind of archaic socialism.

Leadership in the Egyptian bureaucracy did not constitute a "civil service," but a hierarchical ordering of more or less ascribed positions of diffuse status and authority in which incumbents exercised, though not in the differentiated sense of early modern monarchy, the king's authority by virtue of participating at various levels in his charisma.[19] It seems that such participation, as in the case of the priesthoods, was closely assimilated to strict kinship with the royal lineage. However, it is unclear how far this criterion could have been applied exclusively in such a complex system.

Thus there existed a graded hierarchy of service. A religio-civil bureaucracy comprised the higher echelons with some differentiation, but its two aspects were not rigidly distinguished. Officials derived their legitimation and even, more or less formally, their appointments from the king and his high officers. However, the crucial criterion of a developed bureaucracy, a clear legal line between office and other personal statuses, did not exist. Bureaucratic office was a more or less total "status" carrying many residual, non-administrative obligations and privileges, some requiring constant service, others being invoked only on various occasions. Correspondingly, the economic resources needed to conduct offices were more or less centrally provided for, including (evidently without clear discrimination) the personal expenses of the officials and their relevant kin and, perhaps, clients. Both for lack of information and for more positive reasons, we must not exaggerate the degree of this control. The lack of legal limits to official duties did not preclude different groups from having the power to affect the terms of their services, secure exemptions from services, or maintain property interests that were independent of particular official positions.[20] This last point relates to another aspect of fluidity in the system. Evidently, there were tendencies, similar to those found in feudal systems, for certain persons and kinship groups to control multiple offices, often both priestly and civil, and to shift from one type of office to another.[21] Such pluralism generally supports effective checks on central authority. Thus this system, like many others, was far from being immune to "power struggles." [22]

Problems posed by such particularistic "interest" structures become most important at the lower levels of the administration and in local community organizations. Presumably, most craftsmen, temple scribes, and the like, held regular jobs in particular organizations, whether temples, administrative units, or local bodies. Almost certainly these positions were predominantly hereditary,[23] though the situation retained some flexibility. In any case, the masses of the common people were peasants working the land, organized along highly

[19] Frankfort, *Ancient Egyptian Religion, op. cit.*, especially p. 36.
[20] Edgerton, "The Question of Feudal Institutions in Ancient Egypt," *op. cit.*
[21] Wilson, *The Culture of Ancient Egypt, op. cit.*, especially Chaps. IX and X.
[22] S. N. Eisenstadt, *The Political Systems of Empires* (New York: The Free Press of Glencoe, 1962).
[23] Wilson, *The Culture of Ancient Egypt, op. cit.*; also Frankfort, *The Religion of Ancient Egypt, op. cit.*, pp. 33–35.

traditionalized lines. Whether rural or urban, the population was also organized into territories ruled after the model of the pharaonic institution by governors appointed from the local aristocracy by the pharaoh, and responsible to him. Within the territories, however, the national and territorial governments generally operated independently, utilizing separate means of organizational effectiveness.[24]

Thus, Egyptian society contained many bases of solidarity which were independent of and cross-cut the main hierarchy emanating from the divine king. Thus, not all particularistic elements were so thoroughly atomized that the whole society was at the "disposal" of the royal leadership for any tasks that advanced national policy.[25] By modern standards, the possibilities for such mobilization were certainly very limited. However, such qualifications, though important, do not negate the vast difference in capacity for mobilization between Egypt and *any* primitive society. Throughout the society immense human resources could be used for important enterprises so long as the plan could be conceived and implemented largely from the top. The development of such capacity for organized collective effort was something quite new in social evolution. The processes by which collective goals should be determined and collective leadership held responsible presented a new order of social problems, which now become a major concern of this book.

In this light, one may say that the major integrative functions of Egyptian society centered about a scale of stratification which used the royal lineage as its primary reference point. Status in the system, which, as we have seen, involved both general social prestige and authority, was strongly ascribed to kinship in both its lineal and affinal aspects. However, it appears that, because integrative mobility was essential in order to articulate specific statuses with service mobilization, pressures developed that made the affinal structures more flexible than otherwise—certainly more so than in primitive systems. When arranging marriages or making appointments, the high officials of the court and the priesthoods had considerable discretion in choosing among persons whose lineages were approximately equivalent in status.

The stratification hierarchy seems to have had one main functional, as distinguished from hierarchical, basis of differentiation, that between the religious hierarchy of priesthoods and the secular-administrative hierarchy, though this distinction was by no means rigid. This differentiation derived basically from the mode in which the society was involved in the structure of the action system at the most general level, the two hierarchies relating to the society's two primary functional references. One such reference involved managing first the environmental conditions of well-being, focusing on the Nile as the source of agricultural fecundity, and then the instrumental conditions of effective collective action, especially in regard to public order and public works. The other concerned articulation with the society's cultural foundations through the pharaoh's relation to the divine order and the *ritual* management of social and natural processes.

A most striking feature of the Egyptian mode of relating the two hierarchies was the low degree of formalization of the legal system, especially when

[24] Wilson, *The Culture of Ancient Egypt, op. cit.*; Edgerton, *op. cit.*

[25] K. A. Wittfogel, *Oriental Despotism* (New Haven: Yale University Press, 1957), seems to have developed his argument largely from this erroneous viewpoint.

compared to the Mesopotamian codes, which we will discuss later. Justice, though religiously sanctioned in that its ideals were assimilated to the divine order, was the prerogative of the pharaoh and his officials in such a personal manner that the particularities of litigants' statuses were inherently involved in all "legal" action and the few codes were scarcely more than collections of wise decisions.[26]

The religious aspect of the Egyptian system was its most striking feature, "bureaucratic" effectiveness itself depending very considerably on this aspect. Here we return to our keynote: Egyptian kingship was *at the same time* religious and political in a sense entirely foreign to modern conceptions. Pharaoh was a very special kind of god, integral to the divine system. Hence, it is as important to characterize the system of divinity as the king's position in it. Generally, we may regard Egyptian religion as "symbolizing" certain critical features of the human condition, but also as asserting its distance and differentiation from the divine substantially more than even the advanced primitive religions.

Apparently, the central theme affirmed by the religion was the *continuity* of the socio-cultural system, conceived as based on an integration of the divine order, human society, and subhuman nature.[27] Pharaoh, as both king and god (Horus), was the system's integrative center. Both divine and human, he was a crucial link in the continuity of all meaningful phenomena. He was the "son" of Re, the Sun-god believed to be the primary source and ground of all living things. More directly, he was also the "son" of more specific divine parents, the mother-goddess, Hathor, and his own royal father, as symbolized in the equation of Horus and the Bull.[28] Thus his humanity was linked to the general procreative order of animal life. He was also deeply implicated in nature's cyclical processes—the seasons, the planting and harvesting of crops, and the Nile's annual flooding. Moreover, the kingship was a multi-generation institution that linked the living pharaoh with both his ancestors and his successors.[29]

To the psychologically aware, particularly striking is the explicit involvement of a complex incest theme in the procreative order. In general, all religious systems seem to articulate in symbol with a socio-psycho-sexual base. The Egyptian case illustrates this very clearly through the occurrence of the incest theme at two levels. First, Egypt was one of the historic cases in which brother-sister incest in the royal family was mandatory for continuing the royal line.[30] However, the pharaoh and his sister evidently mated only on very formal occasions, and only to secure an heir to the throne. Otherwise, they were sharply segregated. Thus, they certainly were not "married" in the sense of sharing everyday life concerns and placing sexual relations in that context.

[26] Cf. Sabatino Moscati, *The Face of the Ancient Orient* (Garden City, New York: Anchor Books, 1962), pp. 145–146. This means that, in Weber's terms, law was governed by substantive, not formal, rationality, so far indeed as it was specially rationalized at all.

[27] Frankfort, *Kingship and The Gods, op. cit.*, Book I, *passim* and *Ancient Egyptian Religion*, Chap. I; Wilson, "Egypt," *op. cit.*, Chap. II.

[28] Henri Frankfort, *Kingship and The Gods, op. cit.*, Chap. III and Part III, *passim*.

[29] Thus, unlike the Shilluk conception, the death of the pharaoh and the accession of his successor were conceived simply as phases of a *single* indivisible process, precisely on the religious level.

[30] Russell Middleton, "Brother-Sister and Father-Daughter Marriage in Ancient Egypt," *American Sociological Review* (October, 1962), 27:603–611.

Second, however, as Frankfort shows, the incest theme recurred on a more profound symbolical level. Here, on his death, each pharaoh, as the god Horus, eventually became Osiris, Horus' father, who stood for both the divine aspect of the particular king who had just died and *all* the dead pharaohs in Egyptian history collectively.[31] There were two remarkable features of the Pharaoh's symbolic transition from life to death. First, he re-entered the womb of his symbolic divine mother, Hathor. But, concurrently, he procreated in her "supernatural" body the new pharaoh, who, in his divine aspect, was Horus.[32]

On certain levels, then, the continuance of the religious basis of society was grounded in incest. It is a commonplace of modern psychology that brother-sister incest is the least "serious" of the three types possible in the nuclear family, incest between mother and son being the most "serious." It seems significant that the Egyptian system actualized the former institutionally, though mainly in the confined context of assuring a proper royal succession, but yet enacted the latter symbolically to indicate the religious meaning of what Horus was really doing when he became Osiris. Perhaps it was the divine "reward" he received with death in accepting the after-life. In a sense we may, paraphrasing Weber, regard this as the "nonfamilial top" of a kinship-structured upper class, with the pharaoh's incestuous privileges and obligations symbolizing his very special status.[33]

Frankfort warns us not to "rationalize" Egyptian religious symbolism as if it were a philosophical theology—for example, the Egyptian conception that a fetus was the primary procreative agent seems patently irrational to moderns. He suggests that the "logic" of the Egyptian symbolic system is comparable to that of primary process as analyzed by Freud. In any case, the continuity theme has special references to the problem of death and, most importantly, to the king's mortality. The essential symbolic assertion, which seems to be that death was relative to a higher reality in the continuity transcending death, is perhaps characteristic of all religions. But in this case, the pharaoh's special relation to the entire cosmic order lends the assertion meaning at rather unique level.[34]

The conception of this higher reality, however, contrasts sharply with those of "historic" religions, since it emphasizes man's erotic interests and their relation to kinship structure and procreation. The combination of reentry into the maternal womb and incestuous procreation evidently "equated" birth and death symbolically in primarily *psychological* references. There was an exchange; as the old Horus became Osiris, the new Horus emerged from Osiris *cum* Hathor—the *balance continued.* Furthermore, the pyramid-tomb was in part a womb symbol, and mummification symbolized the indefinite preservation of a "life-like" form as a fetus, the state in which human organisms "live" minimally disturbed.[35] The continuity of this equivalence seems to have been the thematic core of the famous cult of the dead—and a clear basis for conflict with the Hebrew orientation discussed in Chapter 6. It did not simply deny

[31] Frankfort, *Kingship and The Gods, op. cit.*, Part II.

[32] *Ibid.*

[33] This is a special case of the very general principle that the origin of a differentiated system must, by *its* standards, be undifferentiated.

[34] Frankfort, *op. cit.*, Parts II and III; and Frankfort, *Ancient Egyptian Religion, op. cit.*, pp. 88–123.

[35] Frankfort, *Kingship and The Gods, op. cit.*

the reality of death—otherwise it would not be authentically religious in our sense—but it clearly asserted the primacy of continuity, not just of the human genetic strain, but also of its *social* organization through psycho-social succession.

This "constitutive cult", that of the continual *re*-creation of psychic and social life, was spun between the components of a conceptual system of order. First, as Frankfort emphasizes, it involved the conception of a "cosmic" just and proper order, termed *Maat*. The basic function of the pharaonic institution was to act in accord with *Maat* and to preserve it through action.[36] Distinctions between active and passive references in this connection do not seem to have emerged clearly. However, it is clear that Egyptian society was permeated with beliefs confirming the enormous importance of maintaining the cult in full elaboration. Hence, to infer that Egyptians believed that failure of the pharaoh and his priests to uphold the cult might jeopardize the cosmic constitution itself is not too far-fetched. Thus, it should be clear that *Maat* was *not* a conception of order like that presumed in modern philosophy, or even the Book of Genesis.[37] It may perhaps be called a "ritual" order, for it contained much more "projection" of human interests and motives than do more advanced conceptions, such as those of the Hebrews and Greeks.

A second aspect of order was in a certain sense "natural." It seems to have involved two major themes, those Frankfort calls "procreation" and "resurrection".[38] The first concerned the relation of human society to the animal world. Here Frankfort emphasizes the importance of cattle and, in that context, points out the close relation between Egypt and the upper Nilotic societies, in which cattle also plays a very crucial religious role.[39] In this connection, Horus and Hathor were symbolized by the bull and the cow. Indeed, syncretism between men and animals was very prominent in Egyptian art. It appears to be important, then, that this theme was intimately related to the erotic complex of the constitutive cult since, in general, animal symbolism is associated with erotically regressive elements in human motivation.

The theme Frankfort calls "resurrection" refers to a complex that centered about the fertility of the soil and the seasonal cycle of the crops. With Egypt's lack of rain, the seasonal cycle, which depended on the Nile's annual flood, was both sharply marked and crucial to agriculture. These conditions were directly integrated into the religion; symbolically, planting the seed represented the "killing" and burying of Osiris, and its sprouting under the flood's stimulus was his "resurrection".[40] Thus, human continuity was grounded in the deepest levels of organic life, the seasonal cycle of vegetation, as well as in the procreative immortality of animal species. The Egyptian ritual system, then, "managed" not only human society, through the pharaoh and the gods, but also its relation to the entire organic world.

I have suggested that the Divine order of Egyptian culture was not "super-

[36] *Ibid.*, especially Part II; Wilson, *The Culture of Ancient Egypt, op. cit.*, Chaps. V and VII.

[37] Kenneth Burke, *The Rhetoric of Religion* (Boston: Beacon Press, 1961), Chap. III.

[38] Frankfort, *Kingship and The Gods, op. cit.*, Part III.

[39] *Ibid.*, Chap. 14; also, c.f., for example, E. E. Evans-Pritchard, *The Nuer* (Oxford: The Clarendon Press, 1940), and *The Divine Kingship of the Shilluk* (Cambridge: The Cambridge University Press, 1948).

[40] Frankfort, *Kingship and The Gods, op. cit.*, Chap. 15.

natural" in the sense even of the divine of early Judaism. Similarly, the procreative and resurrective themes should not be regarded as aspects of an "order of nature" in the sense, for example, of the late Greeks. Egyptian religion does present a roughly conceived hierarchy running from the sphere of the gods, through human society and the higher animals, to vegetation. The ordering of these levels, both internally and in their interrelations, did not, however, achieve a differentiation sharp enough to justify applying the terms supernatural and natural in the sense of Western religion and philosophy.

Eisenstadt has suggested a parallel between Egypt and China, in that both societies, each on its own terms, attained very unusual levels of integration and structural durability.[41] However, I can treat this important subject only after discussing China, for as Eisenstadt emphasizes, the similarities between the two systems are embedded in critical differences regarding developmental level.

The Mesopotamian Empires

Egypt exemplified the more hierarchical type of archaic society, being structured in both religious and secular aspects about a series of ordered gradations from the pharaoh down through a variety of levels. Indeed, the pyramid may serve as a symbol of the structure of the society itself. Though like all societies it was segmented, on geographical (and some other) bases, it is difficult to see how a pattern of association between autonomous, presumptively equal units could be compatible with, or evolve very directly from, such a society.

The Mesopotamian cases present a sharp contrast in precisely this important respect. They exemplified a basic pattern which, in a variety of specific forms, pervaded the whole region from the central Mediterranean through its islands, peninsulas, and coasts, eastward to the valley of the Tigris and Euphrates —namely, the early development of relatively autonomous urban communities. In a sense, the broader, society-wide structures developed by processes of superimposition on, or amalgamation of, these units in such a way that the units themselves were not totally absorbed. This more associative pattern of organization seems to have first attained high development in Mesopotamia, and there achieved a scale and political effectiveness that even went beyond Egypt.

Mesopotamian society lacked the remarkable boundedness and closure which characterized Egypt and, with that, the latter's unusual and long-lasting stability. Certainly, this aspect relates to geographical factors. Though also centering on a river-valley in an arid area, the Tigris-Euphrates region is not so self-enclosed as the Nile region. Society there has a long history of contact, trade, and migration with the societies along the Mediterranean coast, in Persia, and in the Arabian and Syrian deserts.[42] And the delta on the Persian Gulf has always been open to foreign contact by sea.

From very early times, the social structure evidently took the form of multiple city states, or, if not quite that, of relatively autonomous urban communities that controlled the agricultural territories surrounding them.[43] Their dominant elements were sets of upper-class lineages that had relatively equal

[41] Eisenstadt, *op. cit.*
[42] Sabatino Moscati, *Ancient Semitic Civilizations* (New York: Putnam, 1957).
[43] Moscati, *The Face of the Ancient Orient, op. cit.*, Chaps. II and III.

formal status. At one level, formal authority rested mainly in a council of elders comprised of the heads of these lineages.

The more centralized aspects of the authority structure were also rather pluralistic. On the local level there was an even closer integration of functionally diffuse religious and political organization than in Egypt. The gods were conceived to be the ultimate proprietors of the land, a conception institutionalized in that the temples were the major units of economic organization. Apparently, their religious legitimation was the main source of flexibility in mobilizing resources, for allotments were controlled, at least to some degree, by the temple authorities, and manpower was mobilized for various collective projects by temple corvees (labor obligations).[44] These temples were the focus of cults which were not so closely integrated with *specific* social units, either kinship or territorial, as is usual in primitive societies.

Thus, the large city-state was formed by the confederation of *several* land-holding temples, with the largest, presumably that of the main urban center, becoming *primus inter pares*, first among equals. The chief priest of this temple then assumed the position of "governor," and became responsible for the primary instrumental functions of the community, particularly operation of the irrigation systems and the management of trade relations with other communities.[45] The governorship seems normally to have been hereditary in the chief priest's lineage.

The institution of kingship was gradually "superimposed" on this structure. The very early Mesopotamian city-states did not ordinarily have kings. They were elected by the councils of elders only to meet specific emergencies, generally military.[46] Perhaps the governor's religious status made military service unsuitable for him. Here it may also be important that most Mesopotamian city-states were not provided with strong geographical defenses, like the Greek *poleis*, which were situated on islands or small coastal plains surrounded by high mountain barriers. In any case, the early kings were expected to serve only for the duration of particular emergencies. However, situations tended to become defined as continuing emergencies. Gradually, kingship gained permanent and, indeed, hereditary status in particular city-states. Then the many city-states of the valley region were consolidated into empires under numerous dynasties. The institution of kingship, however, continued to bear the imprint of its relatively *ad hoc* origin, which underlies its great differences from Egyptian kingship.[47]

According to our present classification, Mesopotamian society was, however, definitely archaic. Its literacy was clearly confined to the craft level. The close connection between the priesthoods and the management of economic affairs presumably relates to this. Probably the religious and accounting functions involving writing were often performed by the same people.

Mesopotamian society held to a religious primacy very different from any found at later phases of religious development. In the local, city-state organizations, the fusion of political and religious structures was as extensive as in

[44] H. W. F. Saggs, *The Greatness that was Babylon* (New York: Hawthorn, 1962).
[45] *Ibid.*
[46] Moscati, *The Face of the Ancient Orient, op. cit.*
[47] Frankfort, *Kingship and The Gods, op. cit.*, Book II, gives an extensive analysis of these differences.

Egypt (perhaps more so), as symbolized by the governor's status as temple-priest. Though kingship originated primarily in secular connections, its functions also were defined very heavily in religious terms. The king's election was attributed, in the first instance, to the gods themselves. He was the mediator between society and the divine, representing the gods to his subjects and interceding with the gods on behalf of his realm and people.[48] His major duties, then, involved promoting the secular welfare of his realm.

Though it originated in small city-states, the significance of kingship lay in its role in the eventual consolidation of the entire Mesopotamian region into an "empire." Like Greece, Mesopotamia had, antedating the imperial phase, a common culture based on a polytheism which was fundamentally unitary despite local variations. Hence, the great kings were able to become primary mediators between the whole pantheon of gods and all the societies under their domain.[49] No other institutionalized agency could fill this position since the city-states, their temples, and governors were inherently local. Given the general tendency of an archaic society toward religious primacy, perhaps the very strong emphasis on the king's religious functions at the supra-local level is not surprising.

The consolidation of the whole region under a single religio-political system stratified both the religious and the political spheres into a three-level complex in some respects parallel to that of Egypt. We have mentioned that the typical Mesopotamian city-state had a gentry class of secular notables and priests standing above the common people—peasants, artisans, and, with increasingly greater prominence than in Egypt, merchants and traders. Around the king, however, there developed a central priesthood and bureaucracy. As in all archaic societies, the hereditary principle was prominent in this echelon, but evidently there was also considerable scope for a variety of patrimonial relationships.

The development of imperial institutions was accompanied, with what causal relations we do not know, by a generalization of major elements of the cultural tradition, particularly the constitutive symbolism. The status of the king was, as noted, heavily dependent on his religious legitimation by one or more gods in a complex pantheon which had attained pan-societal significance transcending the more local cults, though it seems that the latter continued to exist also. Indeed, they constituted a major source of instability in the larger political structure through the political loyalties they continued to be able to legitimize.

Underlying the kingship, there remained a plurality of local city-states maintaining a basic independence much more thorough than that of the Egyptian territories.[50] This was a basic obstacle to the close integration of the system. No dynasty could secure tight control in the face of so many crystallizing points for new regimes, especially in strategically and economically important cities of historical and religious significance.[51] Need for protection against the

[48] *Ibid.*

[49] Moscati, *The Face of the Ancient Orient, op. cit.* For the continued importance of this, even to quite late times, see A. T. Olmstead, *History of the Persian Empire* (Chicago: University of Chicago Press, 1948).

[50] Moscati, *Face of the Ancient Orient, op. cit.*, and Olmstead, *op. cit.*

[51] Thus, it became usual to change the capital of the empire as new dynasties arose.

fragmentation of their empires was perhaps a major reason why the kings emphasized their religious legitimation so strongly.[52]

Despite this religious primacy, the Mesopotamian kingship was not typically defined as divine.[53] Some kings claimed divinity, but this was limited, sporadic, and, very likely, of dubious legitimacy. Above all, there was no religious sanctification of the royal succession comparable to the Egyptian form. The royal *line* was never conceived to be divine, and sharp conflicts over the succession were frequent; problems of competing lines aside, the many sons of a king with a harem often made considerable trouble themselves. Here, the complete absence of ritual symbolization of royal continuity is particularly important. The funerary ritual for a dead king was completely dissociated from his successor's coronation. This, Frankfort shows, was a major difference from Egypt, where kingship was fundamentally multi-generational.

The important New Year ceremonies also indicate the kingship's lack of consolidation *in* the divine order, compared to Egyptian kingship. These rites were supposed to re-establish the king's solidarity with the divine forces, the yearly renewal of which was conceived as essential to the prosperity of the realm.[54] Here, again, the human order appears contingent on divine favor, rather than integrally involved with the divine order, as in the Egyptian case.

Thus, compared to Egyptian conceptions, there was in Mesopotamia both greater distance between the divine and the human and greater emphasis on *contingency* in the relation between those spheres. If in Egypt the primary royal obligation was to *maintain* the established order of the relationship, in Mesopotamia it was to manage actively an inherently precarious relationship. In this sense, the society lived in a continuing state of religious emergency, fraught with very considerable anxiety, the adequate coping with which was a major duty of the king and the principal base for legitimizing his institutional position. In general, we can consider this a further step in the differentiation of religious and secular spheres.

On the whole, Mesopotamia seems to have attained a higher secular development than Egypt. Although it underwent serious political vicissitudes, including the ascendancy of Sumerian, Assyrian, and Babylonian dynasties and foreign rule under the Persians, this secular development made important contributions to subsequent evolution, particularly in law and trade.[55]

Written legal precepts in Mesopotamia go well back into the third millenium B.C. The code of Hammurabi, the most famous document from the first half of the second millenium, was well foreshadowed by many earlier compilations, and was perhaps not so original as was long assumed.[56] Of course, it was not a code like the *Code Napoleon*, but a survey of legal topics on which,

[52] Olmstead, *op. cit.*

[53] Thorkild Jacobsen, "Mesopotamia," in H. and H. A. Frankfort, John A. Wilson, and Thorkild Jacobsen (eds.), *Before Philosophy, op. cit.*; perhaps Frankfort, *Kingship and The Gods, op. cit.*, Book II, argues this point most fully and persuasively, especially in Chaps. 17 and 19.

[54] Frankfort, *Kingship and The Gods*, Chap. 22.

[55] You will note that these two complexes are located primarily in the integrative and adaptive sectors of the society as a system. The structural emphases of Mesopotamian civilization, thus, contrast with those of Egyptian society, which lay in the pattern-maintenance and goal-attainment sectors. Cf. Chap. 2.

[56] Moscati, *The Face of the Ancient Orient, op. cit.*; Saggs, *op. cit.*

because uncertainties existed, authoritative statements were needed. Hardly a complete "system" in terms of coverage of subject-matter, it did, however, treat a wide range of topics in private law, particularly property and contract and the family. Though not highly generalized in the sense of stating legal principles, it was quite universalistic in applying its rulings impartially to rather wide categories of cases.

Even the earliest Mesopotamian "codes" contained clear legal delineations of fundamental statuses. The basic development that emerged in the successive codes (like that essential to Greek and Roman civilization) was the conception of the free citizen of a city-state, who could hold land and property, enter into contracts and marriages, etc., and expect reliable legal protection as a matter of right. Within the category of free citizens, however, the Mesopotamian codes made systematic class distinctions between members of common and aristocratic lineages regarding legal rights and obligations, especially the punishments and penalties to be imposed upon those guilty of infractions of the laws.[57] The later systems evidently extended the conception of aristocratic status in order to gain higher statuses and greater control over resources for the officials of the imperial bureaucracy.[58] A status of slavery, entered into by capture in war and slave raids or by indebtedness, was also defined legally. In archaic and historic societies substantial parts of what we call the lower class have been slaves.[59] In many respects, this categorization of personal statuses seems to have established a groundwork for that developed by the Mediterranean society of Greco-Roman times.

The concept on which this legal system was based far transcended the idea of retributive justice. The codes contained numerous statements asserting the king's obligation to uphold equitable standards, protect persons in weak positions, and the like. Economic references were particularly prominent, an interesting indication of considerable mobility in economic resources. For instance, the debt relationship was really a salient problem. Clearly, unless resources were emancipated from purely ascriptive embeddedness, no opportunity to "exploit" weaker parties through the debt relationship could arise. Therefore, indebtedness is a definite index of resource mobility under contract, and a probable one of considerable development of money. Concurrent with its enhancement of economic adaptedness, mobility permits "injustices" which, in the sense of the legal documents, could scarcely exist otherwise, however "unequal" ascriptive relations might be. Similar considerations apply to the prominence of family law, which clearly indicated a lack of prescriptiveness in affinal relations.

Evidently, Mesopotamian society also made considerable advances toward establishing procedural institutions. Here, as for other problems, we must allow for variation over a long time and a vast region. Though in the empires justice was ultimately the king's obligation and prerogative, it appears that the city assemblies, presumably consisting mainly of the aristocratic elders, did play an important part, somewhat like modern juries.[60] Sometimes only the assembly's

[57] Moscati, *op. cit.*

[58] Saggs, *op. cit.*

[59] In these, as in other intermediate societies, there were often complex shadings of statuses between members of an indigenous lower class and those who were radically deprived of rights of membership by virtue of being "outsiders" in ethnic or societal community terms.

[60] *Ibid.*

officials functioned, rather than the entire body, and then they are referred to (in translation) as the assembly's "judges." However, there could not have been a fully institutionalized judiciary in the Roman, to say nothing of the modern, sense.

A kind of public law, extending to the "international" field, also developed in Mesopotamia. Indeed, the loose structure of the polity required continuity between "tributary" relations to "vassal" states and "contractual" relations to continguous independent states with which relatively stable ties were maintained.[61] This included various agreements about the rights of trading groups established in, or passing through, the territories, and even the extradition of criminals.

In sum, Mesopotamian society developed a normative order almost verging on the degree of systematization and universalization found in "historic" systems. Its main short-coming was its lack of reference to a unified conception of the grounding of the meanings of the obligations it asserted. In many respects, however, the legal system was the most impressive feature of the society. Mesopotamia had clearly advanced well beyond Egypt in this regard.

Hence, it is not surprising that economic enterprise was considerably developed in Mesopotamian society, going substantially beyond Egyptian levels. This is evidenced by the prominence of contract regulations in the law, by the considerable use of money as revealed by government price-fixing for important commodities, and by the prominence of the indebtedness problem.[62]

Undoubtedly, this trade and its personnel were closely regulated by the government and the temples, but the presence of an important degree of independence seems beyond serious doubt.[63] Money was used in commercial transactions and loans were made at interest, but the very high interest rates suggest that the conditions of security constricted the volume greatly by later standards.

Internal trade was, however, considerable, the rivers being the basic transportation routes. Considering the social and political conditions of the time, the extent of "foreign" trade was quite remarkable. It included both sea trade through the Delta and Persian Gulf and overland trade to Persia, Egypt, and the Mediterranean Coast. Indeed, it seems that through trade many elements of Mesopotamian culture were diffused as far west as Crete, and perhaps even to the Aegean and Greece.[64]

The crucial point here is that, very early and on a large scale, institutionalized market and credit forms of exchange activity developed independence, on the one hand, from the relatively ascriptive and inherently local organization of agricultural and craft production and, on the other hand, from the central government. The fact that they evolved as far as they did is certainly related to the legal developments discussed above. Ventures beyond the ascriptive solidarities that maintained their independence of direct governmental function and mandate were inherently hazardous. Almost certainly this situation could

[61] *Ibid.*

[62] *Ibid.*

[63] *Ibid.*; and Karl Polanyi, Conrad Arensberg, and Harry Pearson (eds.), *Trade and Market in the Early Empires* (Glencoe: The Free Press, 1957). Saggs very seriously criticizes Polanyi's thesis that market economy was virtually absent in Mesopotamia.

[64] Eric Voegelin, *The World of the Polis*, Vol. II of *Order and History* (New Orleans: University of Louisiana Press, 1957), Chap. I; Moscati, *Ancient Semitic Civilizations*, *op. cit.*

not have developed as extensively as it did without legal protection, an arrangement very different from incorporation into the government itself. The development points up very important continuities with Greek and Roman society.

Finally, we may return to the religious aspect of Mesopotamian society. Compared with Egypt, it certainly achieved much greater differentiation between the sacred and secular orders. We have stressed what is perhaps the clearest sign of this, the prominence of *contingency* in the relationship between gods and men. This, in turn, helps account for the prominence of what impresses moderns as "superstition"—for instance, the high development of astrology and the reliance on omens and their priestly interpretations in general—that is, in short, reliance on *magical* components. The essential point here is that the gods' actions were, in sharp contrast to Egypt, conceived as basically unpredictable. As Frankfort puts it, the Egyptians lacked *fear* of god because they were securely embedded in an order so divinely regulated that it only required proper management. For the Babylonians, no such security existed.

Continuing social evolution further involved creating systems of human order able to persist and develop within this basic *contingent* relation between the divine and human conditions.

five

the "historic" intermediate empires

This chapter will discuss briefly four cases or complexes of the advanced intermediate type of society, as defined in the preceding chapter. All developed independent political organizations on a relatively large scale and integrated rather large populations and territories, but they had varying success in achieving stability and maintaining independence.

All of them involved, or depended in some way upon, major cultural developments which separate them clearly from the archaic type of society discussed in Chapter 4. With the possible and partial exception of China, they have all been deeply involved with one or more of the so-called "world religions" in a sense not applicable to any archaic society.

The problems of historical causation concerning the *genesis* of these systems are very complex and lie largely outside the scope of the present discussion. Certain regularities of pattern, both in level achieved and in their ranges of variation, will be the main focus of our concern, along with the problem of why none of these societies, developing upon their own resources, attained what we call modernity.

The systems selected for our study are China, India, the Islamic Empires, and Rome. They will be treated in that order, which is broadly one of progressively greater affinity with the trend toward the modern type. From that point of view, they may also be divided into two parts. China and India were minimally or not at all influenced by the cultural movements which underlay Western society. India was perhaps influenced by Greek culture and certainly by Judaism, via Islam, after the Islamic incursions, but such influences came late in its development. Islam and Rome, however, were very basically influenced by Israel and Greece, respectively. Hence, the problem of distinguishing the themes appropriate to the present chapter from those belonging in the next one is much greater for these two cases.[1]

The societies treated in this chapter were all characterized by the radicalness and comprehensiveness of their *cultural* innovations, centering precisely at the level of constitutive symbolism. They were the immediate loci or direct heirs of the crucial cultural movements which have been called the *philosophic breakthroughs*. The basic common feature of these movements—one that crosscut their very broad differences in orientation—was the attainment of higher levels of generalization in the constitutive symbolic systems of their cultures. This attainment posed critical problems concerning the "coming to terms" of the new cultural orientations with the societal structures in which they arose or to which they were diffused.

It is not necessary for our purposes to analyze the processes which generated these breakthroughs, even to assess the relative roles of various cultural and social factors. It is, however, a salient fact that the breakthroughs occurred within a relatively short time span in several different societies from the eastern Mediterranean (in Greece and Israel), through India, to China. Roughly, the crucial period was the middle of the first millenium, B.C. Our focal concern is with the implications of these changes for institutionalization in large-scale societies—on the scale that the major powers of the time had already achieved. For the breakthroughs of China and India, these implications can be direct; but for those of Israel and Greece, they must concern heir-societies, Islam and Rome being the cases selected in this chapter. The more direct processes in Israel and Greece will be discussed in the next chapter, and the Christian heir-societies will be considered in the sequel book.

In the terms of our analytical scheme, the first major impacts of the cultural breakthroughs—however they may have come about—evidently affected the societal community structures of the societies in which they occurred or to which they were diffused. All these cultural movements developed a differentiation between the order of representations of ultimate reality and the order of representation of the human condition. Any human being's pretension to divine status became out of the question, so that the institution of divine kingship was terminated with the archaic period. But the very sharpness of the newly posed dichotomy between the supernatural and the natural made the problem of defining the relation of human elements to the higher-order reality all the greater and more critical. In general, this underminded the archaic tendency—especially conspicuous in Egypt—to proliferate social status gradations. It tended to introduce a thorough dichotomy between the human elements who have, and those who have not, the capacity and opportunity to act directly in terms of the new conception of the ultimate order. Hence, a new type of *two*-class structuring of the human society seems to be a universal consequence of these cultural innovations. Society comes to be categorized most basically between those who are, actually or potentially, fully qualified for the highest human standing relative to the cultural definition of the transcendent order and those

[1] As a general reference source on these societies, as well as several others (e.g., Persia), see S. N. Eisenstadt, *The Political Systems of Empires* (New York: The Free Press of Glencoe, 1963).

who are excluded from such qualification, either inherently or until (and unless) they meet certain specific conditions of eligibility.

The imposition of this dichotomy upon established societies may involve very complex readjustments. These have worked out in quite different ways in the different cases we will discuss.

One generalization evidently applies to all the societies in which this situation was introduced and in which its institutionalization was attempted on a large scale. There had to be eventual acceptance of the fact that the going society must include major elements who could *not* meet the full criteria of relatedness to the higher order of cultural standards which grounded the cultural definitions of desirable belonging. Chinese society had to include common people who were not "superior men"; India had the *Sudra* and outcastes who were not eligible for the discipline of religious enlightenment; Islam had the infidels who would not convert to the true faith; and Rome had the "barbarians" within her polity. By contrast, a most important trend in modern societies is the presumption of the possibility and desirability of including all persons subject to political jurisdiction in full membership status within the single societal community.

China

Bellah[2] has stated that, among what he calls the historic religions, Confucianism was the most nearly archaic in character. Undoubtedly associated with this is the fact that only in China, among the four cases we will discuss here, did the new cultural level become *fully* institutionalized in a *unified* large-scale society. Furthermore, as we mentioned, China resembled Egypt in its extraordinary basic stability and strong valuation of the bases of stability.

The Chinese Empire took shape about 200 B.C. with its unification under the short-lived Ch'in dynasty and its subsequent consolidation and stabilization under the Han dynasty, which lasted for nearly 400 years.[3] The Han firmly established the first forms of the most distinctive institutions of the Empire, notably the scholar-bureaucracy.

The Empire was preceded by the *Chou* society, a system of patrimonial states resting upon a feudal base. Chou was definitely an archaic society, although it perhaps differed from others in granting a very preferred position to extensive patrilineages, the *Shih*.[4] The prince, like the archaic kings we have discussed, was the senior head of the paramount lineage. Centering about his court, however, there gathered a considerable class of retainers who were not kinsmen, but upon whom he relied for both ritual and administrative services. Furthermore, these men became sufficiently free-floating so that a considerable proportion of them were available for service to different princes moving from

[2] Robert Bellah (ed.), *Religion and Progress in Modern Asia* (New York: The Free Press of Glencoe, 1965), Epilogue.

[3] John King Fairbank, *The United States and China*, 2nd ed. (Cambridge: Harvard University Press, 1959) gives a brief treatment of the essentials of Chinese history, see especially, Chaps. 2–6. More detailed is Kenneth Scott Latourette, *The Chinese: Their History and Culture* (New York: Macmillan, revised 1946).

[4] H. G. Creel, "The Beginnings of Bureaucracy in China: The Origin of the Hsien," in *The Journal of Asian Studies* (February, 1964).

one employment to another as did the men who served different city-states during the Italian Renaissance. They comprised the class of scholar-officials (for whom Confucius, himself, was the most articulate spokesman) who in time came to set the tone for the whole new society.

Such facts reveal that Chou China had become a *system* of partimonial societies which, though warring with one another, maintained a variety of more integrative relations. To a very important degree, they shared a common culture with a common written language and an accumulating body of "classical" documents having both a ritual and a philosophical character. This common culture constituted an esential condition for the establishment of a single politically organized society, the Empire, over such a vast and diverse subcontinental area.

Confucius apparently considered himself to be the codifier of this cumulating written tradition; he denied making any innovations, but wanted only to transmit the "wisdom of the ancients." [5] But, by the very acts of codifying the tradition and adding aphoristic commentaries and observations, Confucius and his followers produced a new level of ordering for the material. Thus, despite its repudiation of metaphysical speculation as entirely vain, Confucianism became a *new* cultural system, one quite legitimately regarded as rooted in a religion.

The Confucian codification became the basis of the famous Chinese classical education. Institutionalizing this education involved the crucial transition from craft literacy to the literacy, in a very distinctive tradition, of a *whole* upper class—i.e., of its adult males. Thereafter, the Chinese "gentleman" was in the nature of the case of a scholar in the Confucian classics.

The institutionalization of the Confucian tradition in an educational system came to include the requirement, firmly grounded in the examination system, that holders of imperial public office (except the emperor himself and certain special categories of courtiers) should be qualified through the discipline of this education—hence, through the societal significance of the cultural tradition, itself.[6] The mandarins, then, became a broad governing class whose status was defined in cultural terms. This was something entirely new in societal evolution. In archaic societies, cultural legitimation was much less independent of the structure of the society. Above all, the impact of the Chinese legitimation system did not concentrate at the top, as, most conspicuously, did the Egyptian system focusing about the pharaoh. The Chinese emperor held only the rather vague "Mandate of Heaven." Rather than integrating the many levels of a cosmos, from the gods to physical nature, as did the Egyptian ruling elements, they imposed a culturally-defined, ultimately-grounded pattern on the society.

To see how this arrangement worked, we must follow two strands outward from the nodal point of the scholar-official's status. The first concerns the nature of the cultural system, itself. The second concerns its mode of articulation in the structure of the society, involving both the positive integration achieved and the limits on such integration.

A major sense in which Confucianism was relatively close to being archaic concerns its involvement with a special conception of boundedness. It held a

[5] Cf. Fung Yu-lan, *A Short History of Chinese Philosophy* (New York: Macmillan paperback, 1962), Chap. 4.

[6] Max Weber, *The Religion of China* (Glencoe, Ill.: The Free Press, 1951), Chaps. V and VI.

notably sinocentric view of the human world and, beyond that, of the whole cosmic system. China was regarded as the "Middle Kingdom," the center of the world. The various systems of order, whether cultural or social, whether general or specific, articulated with, and constituted a set of concentric circles around, this societally manifested center. Yet, in the upward direction, this center was linked to a "cosmic" reference, to the system of a *Tao* and *Yang* and *Yin*, in a manner requiring the ritual management of human relations to these ultimate "forces" or, perhaps better, in Granet's term, "emblems." [7]

The emperor was a kind of pope. He very definitely was not himself divine, but he did hold a divine mandate. His societal functions were much more specifically ritual than those of the pharaoh, leaving much more freedom to his governmental "subordinates." The crucial point seems to be that the supernatural sphere was sufficiently differentiated from the societal order so that it was not necessary to claim direct sanction by the highest legitimating authority for every act of government. The mandarins, as a class, undertook, and were accorded, responsibility for specific governmental acts. They were accountable for the discharge of governmental duties, but they were autonomous in the *way* in which they governed. Heaven, in the Chinese sense, was not a policy-making agency.

The cosmic order and the human social order were conceived to be similarly bounded and essentially congruent with each other through a certain isomorphism or likeness in form. Their principles of order, rather than being rationalistic in the Western sense (i.e., deriving from Greek thought), were symbolic-ritualistic. Order was a matter of the proper relations among diffuse entities defined as being multiply involved with one another. At the cosmic level, the *Yang-Yin* dichotomy was thus identified with a long list of more specific ones—e.g., South-North, Warm-Cold, Male-Female, Upper Status-Lower Status, Left-Right, and so on. *Tao* was the principle of maintaining a proper balance among such entities, with due regard to the various situations in which different ones were predominant and in which cyclical alternation was the important pattern of relationship.[8] To the analytically minded, it is perhaps particularly striking that the dimensions of superiority-inferiority and of qualitative functional difference without hierarchical distinction were not clearly distinguished. *Yang* elements were in general *superior* to *Yin*, as well as being qualitatively different.[9]

In a sense, the main function of the imperial institution was to provide ritual articulation between the cosmic and the human; in this respect it was similar to Egyptian kingship.[10] The human society was organized basically around a *harmony* of differentiated, opposing, and in some way "cooperating" entities. Its order was diffuse and particularistic, with the notable exception of one structural feature, the break between its upper and lower echelons. The social equivalent of *Tao* was *Li*, the observance of proprieties. Each element in

[7] Marcel Granet, *La Pensee Chinoise* (Paris: La Renaissance du Livre, 1934); Fung Yu-lan, *op. cit.*, Chaps. 12 and 15.

[8] *Ibid.*

[9] We will suggest later that such isomorphism between the cosmic and the human social orders and such lack of differentiation are not typical of more advanced socio-cultural systems, but represent aspects of the archaic note in the Chinese system.

[10] Cf. Marcel Granet, *Chinese Civilization* (New York: Meridian Books, 1958), pp. 92 ff., pp. 377 ff.

the society had its proper and appointed place. It should be "given its due" within that place, but, equally, should not be permitted to break away from it.

The institutional embodiment of *Li* was the educated class, particularly its minority that was actually selected for appointment to government offices. As a class, they carried the responsibility for implementing the mandate of the emperor to keep the system in harmonious balance. His was the primarily "ritual" responsibility vis-a-vis the supernatural, cosmic order; theirs was the practical responsibility involving the conduct of human affairs. The two aspects, however, were never sharply differentiated, and the magistrate carried on both practical administrative and ritual responsibilities, linking the locality of his particular office and the society-wide system in both respects.

The social structure, then, interpenetrated with the primary cultural system in a particularly intimate way. The culturally qualified group took over control of the society—on a very imposing scale—in a sense not true of *any* archaic society, by virtue of its embodiment of the ideal cultural patterns. Yet, it could never become the corporate entity which defined the society as a whole, for it was only a body of "superior men" who held a special combination of prestige and governmental authority. But a fundamental line was drawn between them and the "common people," so that classical China remained fundamentally a two-class society. To be sure, it was quite possible for individual sublineages to cross the line through upward (or downward) mobility—and they often did so, though with varying frequency in different periods.[11] In terms of social structure, however, there was never a possibility of including the "lower" groups, especially the peasantry, in the positively valued societal community.

The nature of this class barrier was complex. Fundamentally, it involved China's special approach to kinship, both actually in human society and symbolically in the cultural system. The essential point is that the kinship level of organization was not transcended, as it was in other "historic" systems. To be sure, a main nodal point of the society, the bureaucratic system, involved a special type of universalistic emphasis. Office was open to all who were qualified by education, as tested by the examination system. But this was a "differential joint," the flexibility of which made possible the maintenance of kinship particularism both above and below it in the social structure.

The Confucian ethic established a kind of microscopic-macroscopic congruence between the family and the society as a whole. The famous doctrine of the five relationships included three which were specifically familial—father-son, husband-wife, elder brother-younger brother—all exemplifying the special fusion of hierarchical and qualitative differences mentioned above. (The other two were superior-inferior in official contexts, and friend-friend, one being a "senior" friend who was a kind of patron.) The doctrine held that, if these relationships were properly ordered from the viewpoint of each individual, then the whole society would be properly ordered. Obviously in modern societies the family and its more immediate particularistic environment *cannot* serve as such a prototype of the social structure as a whole.

As a social class, the gentry could not rest solely on its performance of governmental service, partly because of the selective principle in the appoint-

[11] Robert M. Marsh, *The Mandarins: The Circulation of Elites in China, 1600–1900* (Glencoe, Ill.: The Free Press, 1961); Ho Ping-ti, *The Ladder of Success in Imperial China* (New York; Columbia University Press, 1962).

ment system. There had to be more presumptively qualified candidates than offices to fill, otherwise selection of the best would have been meaningless. From the perspective of the individual, the long process of education had to be taken at a risk—he might or might not have a successful career.

Creel claims that the crucial institutional development that marked the transition from *Chou* feudalism to the imperial system was the establishment of the *Hsien*, generally translated as "county" or "district." [12] The *Hsien* was the lowest order unit of imperial administration occupied by an appointed magistrate. For the magistracy and higher positions, the organizational principle was bureaucratic—the encroachment of kinship and other particularistic ties being excluded by quite elaborate precautions, such as the three-year term for holding a particular office and the prohibition against serving in the province in which one's lineage resided.

The town which was the seat of the *Hsien* magistracy was also the residence of the local gentry, who lived in large households with many servants. Typically, their principal economic base rested in proprietorship of agricultural land in the surrounding areas, though many also conducted artisan workshops and mercantile enterprises. They constituted a loose, rather informal corporate group with which the magistrate had to come to terms in implementing policies, and vice versa.[13] That they were town-dwelling, though typically land-owning, made them quite different from mediaeval and post-mediaeval European upper-class groups. In China no "bourgeois" class could become independent of the principal land-owning classes, the "feudal" nobility and gentry, through political control of the towns.

The gentry household, usually called the *chia*, was basically a *three-generation* unit,[14] not a nuclear family household of the modern type. It normally included a parental couple—often complicated by plural wives and/or concubines—their sons, the sons' wives and children, any unmarried daughters, and servants, perhaps including artisans. Particularly important was the institution of basic equality among sons, especially in inheritance—a sharp contrast with the primogeniture of Japan and most of Europe—which was credited to the Han dynasty. On the death of the parents, the sons usually separated, with respect to both the household and its property.

The interposition of *Hsien* magistracies and the equality of inheritance among sons broke the power of "feudal" lineages at the *Shih* level very effectively and made the gentry into an upper *class* much more like the Western than that of any feudal or archaic system. At the same time, the position of the gentry, grounded in both the *Hsien* town and the peasant villages of the countryside, prevented the universalistic bureaucratic institutions from developing effective routine organizational contact with the mass of the people.[15]

For example, taxation was not based upon centrally established rates. Rather, each magistrate was responsible to his provincial governor for a certain sum each year. The taxes were not levied on individuals, but on the *chia* units,

[12] Creel, *op. cit.*

[13] Weber, *The Religion of China, op. cit.*; Chang Chung-Li, *The Chinese Gentry* (Seattle; University of Washington Press, 1955).

[14] Cf. Marion Levy, *The Family Revolution in Modern China* (Cambridge: Harvard University Press, 1949).

[15] Chang, *op. cit.*

and with much "politicking" between the *chia* and the magistrate and among the *chia.* How the magistrate collected taxes from the *chia* and the peasants was up to him, and he defrayed administrative expenses and took his own remuneration from what he could collect.[16] Although he exercised police powers and possibly military enforcement, he had basically to rely upon his working relations with the local gentry both to collect taxes and to secure support and services for governmental operations. They, however, had primary control over the masses of the lower groups, a control which was reinforced by their relations with the governmental system.[17]

The masses of common people were peasants, living in more or less corporate villages and tilling the soil. They maintained the same basic patterns of *chia* organization as the gentry, but usually in truncated form, since economic pressures kept them from establishing such large households.[18] Formally, land could be freely sold or transferred, and the peasants were not serfs, but legally free. Gentry ownership, however, was so widespread that although conditions varied by period and region, large numbers were generally tenants rather than independent proprietors, and, short of tenancy, there was much dependency through chronic indebtedness. Yet, it was possible for peasant lineages to rise into the gentry class through accumulation of landed property. If they had the economic base, they could give their sons a classical education, the great *desideratum,* and adopt the gentry way of life—the scholar's long gown clearly symbolizing that its wearer did not perform physical labor.

The structural importance of kinship particularism was reflected in, and probably much reinforced by, the ancestral cult. Effective solidarity in contexts concerned primarily with the development of instrumentalities (e.g., strictly economic contexts) was never very strong beyond the *chia* level, but more extensive ritual solidarity was maintained through the ancestral system. Since ancestors were in no sense divine in the Confucian system, the Western term "worship" is inappropriate in describing the cult. Rather, the ancestral cult was the basis in ritual propriety (*Li*) for the status of a *chia* unit in the larger system.[19] In more modest ways, the peasants also practiced the ancestral cult.

Creel probably overstates the case somewhat in claiming that the Chinese imperial system developed a full bureaucracy in Weber's sense, though certainly it was very advanced.[20] Perhaps its most important limitation lay in the nature of the qualifications for office (education in the Confucian classics) as compared to the Western traditions of training in the law, with its bearing on organizational competence, or in science-based forms of professional competence. As Weber emphasized, the scholar-official was, above all, a cultivated gentleman, a "superior man" in that sense, not a "professional" in the Western sense.[21]

Nevertheless, the administrative system was the mainstay of an imposing

[16] It was taken for granted that a magistrate would enrich himself as far as possible.

[17] *Ibid.*; Fairbank, *op. cit.*, Chap. 6.

[18] Fei Hsiao-Tung, *Peasant Life in China* (London: Dutton, 1939), and *Earthbound China* (Chicago: University of Chicago Press, 1945).

[19] Cf. Francis L. K. Hsu, *Under the Ancestors Shadow* (New York: Columbia University Press, 1948).

[20] Creel, *op. cit.*; Cf. Max Weber, *The Theory of Social and Economic Organization* (Glencoe, Ill.: The Free Press, 1947), pp. 329 ff.

[21] Weber, *The Religion of China, op. cit.*, Chaps. V, VI, VIII.

socio-political structure which was without peer in scale, stability, and durability until the truly modern era; Rome was comparable in scale, but not in durability and cohesiveness.[22] China proved capable of defense—though it was by no means a highly militarized society. When, as during the Mongol and Manchu conquests, its defenses broke down, it demonstrated its cultural power by very thoroughly Sinifying its conquerors. It mounted vast public works, the Great Wall, canals, palaces, and so on. Yet, China had conspicuous evolutionary limitations in two especially significant fields.

First, rationalization of law and legal procedure was scarcely superior to that of Mesopotamia, and was certainly not comparable with that of Rome. This certainly relates to the character of the cultural tradition. Though *Li*, in one aspect, provided a generalized basis for a kind of law, it was strongly subject to substantive rather than formal rationalization, and was shot through with particularistic themes. This is very evident in Confucius' famous aphorism about the propriety of protecting one's father from the authorities, in the name of filial piety, even though he had stolen sheep.[23]

Second, China failed to differentiate specialized economic structures. Although it achieved relatively high levels of productivity; considerably centralized its resource exploitation, as in the transportation and storage of grain; and probably exceeded Egypt in requisitioning manpower for large enterprises, its economic institutions were highly deficient in two major contexts. The Chinese never developed the monetary institutions necessary to support a highly ramified market system on the scale that the Greeks and Romans did.[24] Also, China did not develop a strong *legally* defined and protected order which could make economic activities relatively independent of requirements for particularistic political protection. In general, only politically powerful groups, as such, could conduct very extensive economic enterprises. Another index of the lack of legal support for economic development was the tendency that emerged whenever central authority was impaired for the economic-political order to break down into "warlordism" and, on a smaller, more local scale, "banditry."

India

The above analysis indicates that the Confucian cultural system and its mode of institutionalization prevented Imperial China from breaking through archaic particularism in reorganizing the society, above all in including the masses of the population in the reorganized system. Weber stated this sharply when he closed his analysis of religion and society in China by contrasting Confucianism with Puritanism: "Confucian rationalism meant rational *adjustment to* the world"; Puritan rationalism meant "rational *mastery* over the world."[25] Confucian adjustment accepted the unalterability of the societal substructure, especially its anchorage in the soil, in primordial kinship relations, and in their cultural accompaniments—above all, magical beliefs.

India's cultural development went much farther than China's in producing

[22] Cf. Eisenstadt, *op. cit.*

[23] Creel has pointed out the significance of this aphorism, *op. cit.*

[24] On the Chinese economy in general, cf. R. H. Tawney, *Land and Labour In China* (London: Allen and Unwin, 1932).

[25] Weber, *The Religion of China, op. cit.*, p. 248, italics added.

a rationally consistent pattern of orientation toward "ultimate reality." It did so, however, in a way that (at least for a very long time) radically dissociated the major modes of implementing the belief system from basic concern with the structure of the society. If Confucianism did not sufficiently differentiate the cosmic order from the social order, Hinduism and Buddhism differentiated them so radically that, in the relevant social conditions, they could not be articulated in a way that would promote progressive institutional change.

In India, a two-class structure much like that of advanced intermediate societies actually preceded, and was clearly important to, the central cultural development. Although an archaic civilization existed in Northwest India previously, the "Aryan" invasions from the North—probably infiltration over a long period around the middle of the second millenium B.C. rather than sudden conquest—brought in a new language, Sanscrit, and a new religion, that centering about the Vedic gods. Both language and religion were certainly related to those of Greece and Rome; they were Indo-European.

Throughout this decisive period, the descendants of the "invaders" comprised the upper group, while those of the indigenous peoples, often called "Dravidian," constituted the lower group.[26] Historically, the class difference included a color factor. As the new religious system developed, the upper group divided into three *varnas*, the Brahmans, the priestly class; the Ksatriyas, the warrior-nobility; and the Vaicyas, the landowners and merchants. Together they constituted the "twice-born," the bearers of the main Vedic cultural tradition who were eligible for its privileged religious statuses. The lower groups, the Sudras, were simply excluded from cultural advantages; they were tillers of the soil, servants, and the occupiers of humble functions and statuses in general. This fundamental division remained essentially constant right down to Ghandi, although the full caste system did not crystallize until after the Buddhist period. For us, the basic duality is more significant than the subdivision of the upper group.[27]

In emphasizing this duality, we are very much aware of the variegated character of the Indian caste system. The main outline, in terms of the three "twice-born" castes, the pure and impure Sudra, and eventually the Untouchables, was relatively clear-cut. However, the effective unit was not the Varna itself, but the caste or subcaste collectivity which was local or at most regional. There was often considerable uncertainty about the exact ranking of such units, especially in the form of regional variations in the ranking of units that claimed to belong to the same Varna. There was also, over considerable periods, an appreciable amount of caste mobility in the Varna hierarchy, usually accompanied by Brahmanic genealogies that were often of dubious authenticity. By and large the system was "tightest" at the top and became looser as one descended the status-scale, at least down to the line between the Sudras and the Untouchables, the latter being totally excluded, in that respectable Brahmans would perform no ritual services at all for them. Our basic point, then, is not that Indian caste presented a neatly polarized two-class system, but that the duality which was central to its religious legitimation was never

[26] Charles Dreckmeier, *Kingship and Community in Early India* (Stanford: Stanford University Press, 1962).

[27] Max Weber, *The Religion of India* (Glencoe, Ill.: The Free Press, 1958), Chap. I.

transcended in the direction of the inclusion of the nonprivileged in a more equalized societal community.

The Vedic religion centered not only on a polytheistic pantheon, but also on a sacrificial cult which shared many features with the cults of Mesopotamia and Palestine. The Brahmans were its priestly group, functioning about the sacrifice. But the distinctive cultural development was the philosophical speculation about the meaning of the sacrifices in which they engaged, along with the nonpriestly Aryans.[28] From this speculation came the conception that the world of life consisted of a myriad of timeless, metaphysically ultimate entities, or souls, undergoing an endless series of incarnations and reincarnations. Not only was individual death (or birth) not considered ultimate, but everything terrestial was radically relativized. The whole world of zoological life—why plants were excluded is mysterious—was comprised of incarnated souls, not only of man, but of all species, even the lowliest insects or worms. Above man was the realm of the gods, who were also mortal incarnations of souls, though perhaps living for thousands of years. Only souls and the ultimate "grounds" of being of the universe, Atman or Brahman, were exempt from mortality and relativity in this sense.

The ultimate meaning of temporal process was formulated in the concept of moral causation, *Karma*, according to which the consequences of every act of every living being was indelibly attributed to the responsible individuals. On this basis, souls were thought to be rewarded for meritorious acts by being promoted on the scale of being for their subsequent lives, and punished for reprehensible acts by being demoted. Quite clearly this system was inherently hierarchical, ranging from the gods, through the gradations of human society, to the lower animals.[29]

Such radical relativization raised acutely and centrally the problem of the meaningfulness of the individual human life. This problem was addressed through a doctrine of radical salvation.[30] The religious goal was to go beyond optimizing one's fortunes in the round of rebirths and to escape completely from the "wheel of karma," attaining some kind of absorbtion into the ultimate.

Besides its extreme philosophical sophistication and generalization, two features of this religious orientation have special significance for our immediate purposes. First, given that the highly cultured Indian was permeated with these beliefs, and that he would hence desire to seek radical salvation, the character of the orientation precluded his doing so in the ordinary course of secular life. The path to salvation lay through withdrawal from secular associations and responsibilities and practice of ascetic exercises or mystical contemplation. As Weber strongly emphasizes, there was no equivalent of the Confucian valuation of the ethical obligations of public life, to say nothing of a Puritan-type conception of the *calling*. To be sure, social responsibility was religiously sanctioned, but as *second* best, not as a prime obligation of life.

Second, the doctrine was *radically individualistic* at the religious level. There was no pattern of a collectivity parallel to the "People of Israel" or,

[28] W. T. de Bary, S. N. Hay, R. Weiler, and A. Yarrow (eds.), *Sources of Indian Tradition* (New York: Columbia University Press, 1958), Chap. 1, especially pp. 15–18.

[29] Heinrich Zimmer, *Philosophies of India* (Cleveland: Meridian Books, 1956).

[30] Weber, *The Religion of India, op. cit.*, Chaps. IV and V.

especially, the Christian Church. Each person sought his salvation entirely on his own, with the tutelage of a particular spiritual guide, a *guru*.

Underlying these two characteristics was the main purport of the doctrine, the devaluation of life in this world. In the extreme form in which it was developed by certain of the philosophical schools, this involved the conception that concrete existence was itself wholly an "illusion" (*maya*), and that appreciation of "reality" was possible only through turning one's back on "the world."[31]

The consequences of such a view depend very much on the conception of the nature of "the world." In the relevant periods of Indian history, concrete human society clearly had to be decisively *devalued*, though in a relative sense, to be sure. Weber's thesis, then, I find incontrovertible: that, in the circumstances, this meant *traditionalized*. However, the very fact that Brahmanic religion was not radically ascetic for the ordinary man, but only for the "religious virtuoso," is quite important in respect to the viability of this traditionalizing ethic.

The society in which this new cultural movement developed was apparently a relatively advanced archaic society, not terribly different from that of Mesopotamia. There were patrimonial principates, capital cities of considerable size and complexity, a high development of craftmanship and of certain arts, public works on a large scale. Since both the time period and the variation at any given time were considerable, any such characterization must be very general. Indeed, continuity and communication with Mesopotamia, via Persia, was probably very important. The essential question is why, in a broad area of roughly comparable social conditions, the constellation of factors necessary for further societal evolution came together on the western periphery, but not on the eastern periphery.

Whereas Confucianism consolidated and advanced the *cultural* institutionalization (in the cybernetic sense, control) of the Chinese social order, the Indian religio-philosophical movement, which in cultural terms was far more advanced than Confucianism, drained away cultural impetus for social development, leaving the society at the mercy of relatively archaic social configurations.

Developing in the upper classes, with special reference to the Brahmans, the cultural movement became highly complex, particularly in its involvements with the cultural system, and divided into three major branches in the "classical" period—Hinduism, Jainism, and Buddhism—all of which departed from common ground. Jainism developed a very solid position as a sectarian subgroup within the society, in some respects parallel to that of the Jews in the Diaspora, though not nearly so wide-spread. As Weber pointed out, it was particularly important as the basis of a commercial class.[32] Buddhism, broadly the most radical of the three religions, was completely extruded from India, but became one of the three most important proselytizing religions in world history, extending throughout the whole of Asia south and east of India, though it did not fully displace indigenous culture in China and Japan.[33]

[31] *Ibid.*; also Max Weber, *The Sociology of Religion* (Boston: The Beacon Press, 1963), Chaps. IX–XII; and Zimmer, *op. cit.*

[32] Weber, *The Religion of India*, *op. cit.*, Chap. VI.

[33] Cf. Hajime Nakamura, *Ways of Thinking of Eastern Peoples: India, China, Tibet, Japan* (Honolulu: East-West Center Press, 1946).

Hinduism, led by the Brahmans, became the predominant basis of the later cultural and organizational framework of Indian society. But, instead of promoting a corporate societal collectivity of the "twice-born", which could then be extended to include the whole society, it consolidated the religious other-worldliness and individualism of the general Indian tradition at the societal community level. This powerfully legitimized a fragmented hierarchical order of secular society on the religious level. Thus, secular society was regarded as the human arena for the operation of *karma* and transmigration in such a way that merit relative to *karma* coincided with *dharma,* the performance of the traditional obligations of caste status.[34] The individual was a "good citizen" insofar as he observed the traditional obligations of his ascribed station in life. If meritorious, he would move upward in the *next* incarnation; otherwise, downward. The main social structure, then, was one of hereditary groupings, largely occupational, but with cross-cutting "tribal" divisions and with village communities which symbiotically included members of a number of castes and provided a framework for broader organization in the largely agrarian society. The criteria of status, not in but *of* the caste, were overwhelmingly ritual criteria in terms of the Brahmanic conception of the world. For these reasons, the Hindu orientation could not possibly legitimate any major movement for social change.

The system for attaining salvation articulated with the *dharma* system through the institutionalization of other-worldly asceticism and mysticism on an individual basis. Ideally, the high-caste individual was to pursue radical other-worldiness in the later stages of his life, after he had met his traditional obligations and left a son old enough to continue the kinship line.[35]

Hinduism consolidated only after the rise of the Buddhist movement, which was still more radical in devaluing life in this world in favor of contemplative-mystical withdrawal. Buddhism did not sanction caste after the Brahman manner, but treated all secular affairs as of little consequence. It did develop a collective structure, a form of monastic community, the *Sangha,* in which monks lived together in withdrawal from the world. But its sense of religious community did not extend to the ordinary person; there was no Buddhist parallel to the Christian laity. Moreover, its monastic life was radically dissociated from any social usefulness. This applied even to the monks' maintenance—the strict monks could not even grow their own food, but had to beg for it, since work was defiling.[36]

It is striking that no long-term, stable, large-scale political organization was established on the Brahmanic base. Although India developed many principalities and kingdoms, only one primarily Hindu empire gained considerable size and duration, during the Gupta dynasty of the fourth century, A.D.

There was, however, a very notable *attempt* at political consolidation under the famous king, Ashoka, of the Maurya dynasty (fourth century B.C.). Although Ashoka eventually joined a Buddhist monastery, he was not really a Buddhist.[37] Rather, he attempted to mold a general social order (his system of

[34] Weber, *The Religion of India, op. cit.*; Zimmer, *op. cit.*

[35] Zimmer, *op. cit.*; and de Bary, *et al., op. cit.*, Part III.

[36] *Ibid.*, Chaps. VI and VII; also Nakamura, *op. cit.*

[37] Peter Pardue, "The Enigma of the Ashoka Case" (Harvard Doctoral Thesis, 1965); also A. L. Basham, *The Wonder That Was India* (New York: Macmillan, 1954).

Dhamma) by syncretizing various elements of the whole tradition, Brahmanic, Buddhist, and Jain. This was as near to a general upper-class culture similar to Confucianism as ever appeared in Indian history.

Significantly, Ashoka's synthesis disintegrated both politically and culturally very rapidly after his death. After that, the consolidation of Hinduism and the caste system proceeded apace under strong leadership from the Brahmans who, as a group, had reacted strongly against Ashoka. The Buddhist movement gradually weakened and was eventually extruded from India.

It seems significant that, some centuries later, the Islamic movement spread into India on a grand scale. With varying comprehensiveness and duration, some extensive political structures emerged under Muslim rule. The last and greatest was the Mogul Empire, which controlled virtually all of India for about two centuries prior to the advent of the British. In fact, her history indicates that India was particularly vulnerable to foreign rule. Nevertheless, the Muslims did not manage to convert the majority of India's population to Islam, but had to accept a compromise (as it also did elsewhere) between an Islamic minority and a Hindu majority.[38]

The Islamic Empires

In China and India, the *decisive* cultural developments were directly indigenous to the societies in which they evolved and on which they had their very different kinds of impact. In the Islamic societies and Rome, this was not, in the same sense, the case. Though Islam arose about a millenium after the prophetic age of Israel, and several centuries after the beginning of Christianity, it was, nevertheless, a product of the same broad Semitic cultural traditions.

Similarly, the crucial flowering of Greek culture had come and gone some three centuries before Roman political authority penetrated its area, enabling it to become so strongly influential on Roman society. However, Rome's distinctive development depended less directly on the Greek heritage than did that of Islam on the Israelitic heritage; it was very largely a case of independent variation from a common base, the *polis* system.

Islam and Rome, following Israel and Greece, both developed a pattern of societal community that contrasted sharply with the patterns found in the Orient.[39] In this pattern, the membership of the community was not a class in

[38] I cannot here follow the very complex history of Buddhism outside of India. In light of our discussion of China, however, it may be noted that Buddhism exerted considerable influence there, but only after the Empire was thoroughly consolidated. Although Buddhism, somewhat like Taoism, played an important part in China, it never threatened to displace Confucianism as the main cultural focus of the society. It evidently served an interstitial, "safety-valve" type of role. For example, it was at times particularly prominent at the imperial court, and, more generally, among upper-class women. For many groups, it was closely associated with the circumstances of death, with funerals and memorial observances of various kinds. The differences between the kinds of resistance to full institutionalization, of Buddhism in China and of Islam in India, are suggestive of the differences both between the religions and the societies involved. On the diffusion of Buddhism, see Nakamura, *op. cit.*; Robert N. Bellah, *Tokugawa Religion* (Glencoe, Ill.: The Free Press, 1959) contains an important discussion of Buddhism in Japan.

[39] Max Weber, *The City* (New York: Collier Books, 1962).

the sense of the Chinese gentry or the Indian "twice-born," but the *entire* corporate entity which bore the main cultural tradition.

In early Israel, this entity was the *Chosen People,* corporately bound together and to Jahweh by the *Covenant.* Its members maintained various complex relations with non-members, but the concept, People of Israel, always remained the central reference point for their sense of societal belongingness.

In Greece and Rome, the corporate body of the city-state, *polis* or *urbs,* comprised the focal societal community, the essential category of membership being the status of *citizen.* This body often maintained complicated relations with non-citizens, both within and outside the territorial limits of the city-state, but still it remained the focal entity of the society.

In both the Semitic and the Greco-Roman cases, the crucial community entity was *potentially* a total independent society. This was not so for the upper classes of either China or India. Furthermore, by the nature of their cultural traditions and their societal communities, these Western societies were oriented much more actively than the Oriental societies toward institutionalizing the primary value-patterns of their cultures as constitutive of the society itself—and as a whole.

Islam recognized its cultural derivation from Israel by acknowledging the validity of the major Hebrew prophets, especially Abraham and Moses, and even Jesus.[40] It also had the same basic character of an associational societal community. Originally, this centered on the leading lineages of Medina and Mecca which acknowledged Mohammed's leadership as the true prophet of the one true God, Allah. This community, whose members were at once *believers* and solidary with each other through their common allegiance, was the *Umma.*

From the beginning, it was both a religious and a political community.[41] But, unlike early Israel, it did not for long claim jurisdiction over a traditionally settled territory or population. It began to expand very early, first over the Arabian peninsula and then outside it. Particularly crucial, then, was the question of the relation between the full members of the religio-political community and the non-members on whom it impinged. In general, this was defined neither in terms of class status in the Confucian manner, nor in terms of special religious qualifications in the Brahmanic manner, but was essentially a matter of accepting the faith and giving allegiance to Allah, and his Prophet, Mohammed.[42] Those who did not were infidels, and could not be granted the privileges of the faithful. This is the special Islamic version of the two-class system.

One difficulty became increasingly salient for Islam as it expanded its rule with extraordinary rapidity over a very large part of the civilized world. This was the problem of combining under unified rule the two main aspects of the Islamic community, the *Umma* of the faithful and the political, territorial community. In the first phase of expansion, Arab ethnicity and language provided a certain basis of unity, but thereafter the tendency to identify Islam with Arab

40 H. A. R. Gibb, *Mohammedanism* (New York: Galaxy Books, 1962), especially p. 50.

41 *Ibid.,* Chaps. 2 and 3.

42 Cf. Reuben Levy, *The Social Structure of Islam* (Cambridge: Cambridge University Press, 1962), especially the Introduction and Chap. I. Levy's discussion shows this pattern to have been by far the predominant tendency, despite difficulties of institutionalizing it that sometimes led to hedging on the simple principles of inclusion.

culture became a major hindrance in integrating non-Arab populations into the community.[43]

Mohammed had envisioned a single *umma* which was also a single politically organized society. With Islam's expansion, however, this ideal failed to be implemented in two principal ways. First, it proved impossible to convert all the masses of the conquered populations to Islam, while at the same time maintaining adequate political control *over* them. Almost everywhere (as we have already noted for India), large non-Muslim population elements remained, and, over time, consolidated their positions as non-Muslim, so that gradually all realistic hope of their conversion had to be abandoned.[44] Furthermore, there was a great deal of relatively nominal, "diluted" Islam containing religiously dubious strains of other traditions.[45]

Second, it proved impossible to maintain political unity. Under the strain of its rapid spread, the Islamic system broke up into a plurality of politically independent units by a process somewhat analogous to that which occurred in Western Christendom when the nominally unitary Holy Roman Empire fragmented into feudal-national states. Thus, the Moorish, the Arab, the Persian, the Indian, and eventually the Turkish political systems became independent.

Muslim theory required that there be a single religious head, a successor to the Prophet, who should also wield political supremacy over all Islam. The institution of the Caliphate, however, was never adequately stabilized, but became the subject of rival claims and the occasion of many intra-Islamic wars over a period of several centuries. At issue were competing principles of legitimation, which, though based upon differing claims about descent from the Prophet, involved some very fundamental normative problems which were never authoritatively resolved.[46]

Islam, like Israel, greatly emphasized the religious *law*. It was preeminently a religion of the *Book*, the *Qur'an*, the revealed word of Allah through the Prophet, supplemented by what were traditionally regarded as his sayings, the *Shari'a*, and the interpretive glosses of many generations and differing schools of legal experts. Indeed, the rigid monotheism of Islam strongly inhibited concern for theological subtleties and placed the emphasis in religious culture on the law. Furthermore, the law certainly became the most important basis of unity for the religious community, as indeed it became for Israel.

In two respects, however, Islamic law failed to develop the kind of basis for a normative order that, we shall see, developed in Rome. First, Islam had no clear-cut corporate body to which the authoritativeness of its law referred, not even a people in the Hebrew sense, since it had basically abandoned its ethnic identification with its expansion, though certain aspects of Arab primacy lingered on informally. In general, the law was strictly universalistic in applying ideally to all the faithful equally. But in the absence of a corporate reference, it had to rest on the rather loosely integrated tradition of the *Qur'an*, the *Shari'a*, and the glosses. Although it was maintained by a group of experts, they never

[43] Cf. Gustave E. von Grunebaum, *Medieval Islam* (Chicago: Phoenix Books, 1961), especially Chap. VIII.

[44] *Ibid.*, Chaps. V and VI.

[45] Cf. Clifford Geertz, *The Religion of Java* (Glencoe, Ill.: The Free Press, 1960).

[46] Grunebaum, *op. cit.*, Chap. V.

held an organized status in a corporate entity in the fashion, for example, of the canon lawyers in the Mediaeval Christian Church.[47] This condition permitted the group of legal experts, and actually the law itself, to fragment into several rather diverse and competing schools, thereby making the authoritativeness of legal controls still more problematical.[48] But the underlying difficulty was that the *Umma* did not comprise a corporate entity in, for example, the Christian sense.

Second, Islamic law remained legal*istic* in the sense true of the Jewish law, especially in its Talmudic phase. The *Qur'an* and, even more, the *Shari'a* were very aphoristic and unsystematized. The Islamic tendency was to elaborate particular precepts and prohibitions on relatively *ad hoc* bases, adapting them to the exceedingly various circumstances in which the faithful found themselves. Thus, Islamic law was characterized by ingenious casuistry rather than integration about clearly formulated legal principles;[49] compared to the Roman use of the conception of natural law, it had hardly any philosophical grounding at all.

Indeed, as Gibb emphasizes, it seems that a basic dualism was never successfully transcended and became a central characteristic of all Islamic societies. On the one hand, legitimized by the religious mission of Islam, was a continual drive to unify all the faithful politically. But, on the other hand, was the lasting anchorage of the Islamic masses in traditional agrarian or nomadic societies, organized about kinship and particularistic local solidarities which were never thoroughly structured to match the religious universalism—or even that attained, at times, by the highest political authorities and the law. Indeed, the particularism often penetrated the higher echelons.[50]

Religiously, this basic duality was especially clear. On the one hand, orthodox Islam adhered to a theological rigorism which could not legitimize any mediation with the diversity of human interests and motives. On the other hand, these human elements gave rise to the widespread and popular Sufist movements which fostered an extreme emotionalism, mysticism, and magic that undermined the institutionalization of any distinctively Islamic pattern in large-scale societies.[51]

Besides the heritage it shared with Israel, Islam also came into intimate contact with the heritage of classical antiquity. It was from the Arabs that many classical texts, such as those of Aristotle, were recovered in the West, and in such fields as mathematics they advanced classical culture considerably. Indeed, the impact of the classical heritage gradually led to a major crisis in Islamic culture, reaching its climax with the work of Al Ghazzali, the "Thomas Aquinas" of the Islamic Middle Ages. The basic response to this impact, however, was the opposite of that which prevailed in Christian Europe. Islamic orthodoxy, in protecting the purity of the Prophet's tradition, failed to exploit classical

[47] *Ibid.*; and Gibb, *op. cit.*, Chaps. 6 and 7.

[48] In turn, this made differentiation among the political, religious, and legal foci of societal organization still more difficult.

[49] *Ibid*; and Levy, *op. cit.*, Chaps. IV and VI.

[50] Cf. Eisenstadt, *op. cit.*

[51] On the general point of such dualism particularly, but also for the whole sketch on Islam, I am especially indebted to the work of H. A. R. Gibb. See especially his recent volume, *Studies on the Civilization of Islam* (Boston: Beacon Press, 1962).

philosophy as a means of integrating secular culture into its system, and thereby cut itself off from another basic constituent of modern societies.[52]

Unlike China and India, Islam developed a radically activistic orientation. Acting upon a culturally defined base, it attempted to transform human society into a religiously ordained ideal pattern. It must, then, be judged an historical failure in that it did not even thoroughly Muslimize much of the population under its political control; the relatively complete Christianizing of Europe offers a strong contrast. Beyond that, its cultural tradition and societal normative order did not undergo the crucial processes of differentiation, inclusion, and upgrading that could have transformed the *Umma* into a total society permeated by universalistic norms. Hence, rather like China and India, but in a special sense, the Islamic societies remained, despite their imposing achievements, generally traditionalistic and segmented into a great variety of particularistic groupings operating under a relatively thin veneer of common Islamic culture.

Perhaps the most striking adaptive shortcoming of the Islamic societies was the failure of the *Umma* to become *institutionalized* as a fully corporate societal community, comprising essentially the whole population of the society. Certainly this can be partly attributed to Islam's tendency to direct action—i.e., to take political control, usually through military means, and attempt to "Muslimize" the society from that vantage point. In the sequel volume, we will stress the immense difference between this process and that which set the basis of modern Christian society.

Certain features of the religious tradition itself seem to be the major factor underlying Islam's evolutionary limitations. Islamic monotheism, despite its purity, was embedded in a good deal of archaic cultural content, particularly in the *ad hoc*, unsystematized Koranic law, much of which was parochial to Arab culture or even idiosyncratic to Mohammed, himself. Perhaps still more fundamental, however, was the lack of a philosophical grounding for both theology and law. In its *use* of philosophy, Islam was not on a level comparable with the Indian religions or Christianity. Thus, despite the majestic transcendence of the conception of Allah, the line between the worldy and the other-worldly was not clearly drawn, but somewhat resembled the pattern common in archaic religions.[53] For example, the pleasures of the Harem seem to have been disproportionally prominent in the Islamic conception of the after-life. Its inability to accept the rationalizing resources of Greek culture probably made the full institutionalization of Islam's activistic ideal patterns impossible, insofar as that can be attributed to any single factor.

The Roman Empire

Roman society, in common with the Greek *poleis*, surpassed the Israelitic conception of the People and the Islamic conception of the *Umma* in developing a pattern of societal community having a specifically *corporate* character. Resting on the wide-spread, ancient traditions of city-state organization, the Greek and Roman city-states developed as small, politically

[52] Bellah emphasized this point in a personal communication. It is evident at many points in E. I. J. Rosenthal, *Political Thought in Medieval Islam* (Cambridge: Cambridge University Press, 1958).

[53] Grunebaum, *op. cit.*, Chaps. III and IV.

independent, territorial units, the original cores of which were evidently comprised of aristocratic partrilineages. The heads of these lineages—e.g., the original Roman *paterfamilias*—were presumptive equals *associating* themselves, their kinsmen, and their "clients" into a corporate entity, the *polis* or *urbs*.

In Rome's early phase, before its major political expansion, the originally aristocratic structure of the *urbs* was "democratized," a process common to most of both Greece and Italy.[54] The distinction between patricians and plebians was deprived of certain significances in favor of a common *citizenship* status in which all adult males were presumptive equals. Certainly a very important focus of this development, in both Rome and Greece, was the common involvement in military service—the citizen body (i.e. corporate Rome) *was* also (did not "have") an army. It also established a complex system of elective offices, a citizen assembly with political power, and a universalistically selected senate composed of former magistrates. Although the population governed by the community of Rome did not consist only of citizens with full political rights and their families, these did comprise the core of the societal community in a sense elsewhere true only in Greece and, partially, in Israel.

Not only a corporate citizen body and elective office, but also an effective, authoritative law were characteristic of Rome from an early stage. The legal system underwent a complex internal development somewhat parallel to that of the political system, especially in the extension of legal rights from the *paterfamilias* as a lineage head to the individual male, who became *sui juris* (possessed of full legal capacity to act in his own behalf).[55]

Like early Islam and many other empires, this originally very small corporate society embarked on a career of expansion, successively "conquering" its more immediate neighbors, the whole of Italy, and virtually the whole Western civilized world, including the entire Mediterranean Coast and extending as far as Britain in one direction and Mesopotamia in the other. With this immense territory, the early Empire comprised a population estimated at about 60 million,[56] which was very large indeed for the time.

Rome's vast expansion, from the late Republic on, cannot be explained solely by her superior military organization. However important that may have been in initially taking over new populations and territories, the stabilization of Roman rule was highly dependent on the legal system which provided its institutional framework. It is surely important that, by the time this occurred, Roman law had been greatly systematized upon the principles of the Stoic philosophy of the law of nature. In particular, the *jus gentium* (see p. 88) and the Roman concept of empire itself could not have developed without this philosophical grounding and systematization.[57]

Thus, by utilizing the principles of Greek philosophical generalization,

[54] Cf. William Warde Fowler, *The City-State of the Greeks and Romans* (London: Macmillan, 1921) for a brief treatment of the political and legal aspects of the democratization process.

[55] This, we may note, carried the "de-institutionalization" of kinship solidarity one step farther than the Chinese system did. The male head of the nuclear family household, not merely the 3-generation *chia*, became *sui juris*.

[56] Cf. Adolf Harnack, *The Mission and Expansion of Christianity* (New York: Harper Torchbooks, 1962), p. 8.

[57] Cf. Ernest Barker, "The Conception of Empire"; and F. de Zulueta, "The Science of Law," in Cyril Bailey (ed.), *The Legacy of Rome* (Oxford: Clarendon Press, 1923).

the Roman system of legal order came to be formulated in terms of universalistic principles, applicable to all men and grounded in general views of normative order which could be institutionalized as common to the whole civilization of classical antiquity. The religion of early Rome itself was relatively parochial and archaic and could not alone have developed and legitimized such a legal order. The contrast between Rome and Islam with respect to legal rationalization brings out the great importance of this feature. It was essential to Rome, not only for its ordering of relations among private parties, but also—probably more so—for the constitutional capacity it gave the Roman state to mobilize resources and act with relative rationality and consistency in quite various contexts.

Whatever may be said about the "justice" or humanitarianism of Roman rule, it certainly had unique, historically critical, institutional features. As a "conqueror," Rome did not simply "rule over" its subject peoples in an "imperialist" manner, but in an extraordinary way accepted progressively broader elements of them into her own corporate structure. The most important aspect of this process was the extension of Roman citizenship, first to elite elements and then to more common people; first in Italy, then in Greece, Gaul, Spain, North Africa, the Middle East, and so on. Finally, all free men of the Empire were accorded citizenship, though its significance had by then become so diluted as to be almost meaningless politically. A very important means of extension was the grant of citizenship to all men, whatever their origins, who had honorably served a six-year term in the legions. This was a crucial process of democratization, for it cut across the internal stratification of the subsocieties involved.

Extension of citizenship involved, *ipso facto*, the extension of the "rule of law," because the central legal system, the *jus civilis*, applied to all citizens, whether resident in Rome or not. Furthermore, the legal tradition was so strong that an additional system of law, the *jus gentium*, was developed for the "peoples" under Roman jurisdiction who were not citizens, in order to regulate their relations with Roman authority and with one another.[58] The *jus gentium* articulated with the central law and, hence, extended a set of highly universalistic regulations to the whole population under Roman rule. These concerned, above all, the rights of persons vis-à-vis government and in relation to one another in the fields we would call civil rights, property and contract, freedom of movement, and the like.

Besides the system of substantive rules, Rome also developed an elaborate system of judicial procedure. The principal courts were presided over by the *praetors*, who were not legal professionals, but regular magistrates engaged in political careers. In the later period, however, there did appear legal professionals, the jurisconsults, who advised clients and judges about technical points of the law but were not regular attorneys in the modern sense.

This was by far the most highly developed, largely secular system of law that evolved in *any* society until early modern times. Under its governmental and legal system, Roman society became the most cosmopolitan and individualistic up to its time. Both persons and property enjoyed relatively free mobility throughout the Empire. An elaborate money, credit, and markets institutional complex encouraged the development of relatively non-political economic enterprise. In the more cultural spheres, given the ethnic and cultural heterogeneity of the population, there was an immense range of religious and cultural freedom

[58] Zulueta, *op. cit.*

and mobility. Quite probably, a movement like Christianity could not have spread through proselytization in most other advanced intermediate, to say nothing of archaic, societies. Thus, its legal system, rather than its sheer political control of large territories and populations, was probably Rome's most imposing and distinctive achievement.

In the course of Rome's expansion, its central complex of citizenship and law encountered difficulties in meshing with the rest of the social structure in two, or possibly three, main contexts. First, under Roman conditions, the extension of citizenship in the legal context had to involve a concomitant dilution of its political content. Expanded Rome *could not* function as a political democracy. There are many reasons for this, perhaps especially Rome's failure to develop *representative* institutions. But, in turn, that involved a variety of complex factors, notably the unitary character of governmental authority, the *imperium,* to be discussed presently.[59] In any case, effective political power and influence came to be concentrated, for the most part, in a small upper group, the senatorial class.[60] It also became subject to relatively arbitrary intervention by military elements, not only because of the sheer importance of the military establishment, but also because military units were traditionally units with political powers, as such. When the tendencies to concentrate power eventuated in a monarchy, Rome never managed to institutionalize a stable solution to the crucial problem of succession.

Political concentration was closely related to stratification, though by no means identical with it. The senatorial class became, *de facto,* mainly hereditary, though it remained open to "new men," especially from the provinces. Along with some auxiliary groups, like the tax farmers, the senatorial class came to amass, especially for political use, vast concentrations of influence, power, and wealth, for which there were apparently no very effective countervailing or moderating means of control. This could only tend to erode the position of the Empire-wide citizen body as the core community of the society.

Finally, given the nature of the indigenous Roman religion and the cultural diversity of the Empire, the very development of a secular law and a political authority administered with relative impartiality over so many different ethnic, cultural, and religious groups necessarily generated a crisis in cultural legitimation. The "Imperial cult" was relatively weak, for the cultural sophistication of the Empire had long passed the stage of god-king. Yet, the Empire had developed no adequate alternative for meaningfully articulating the *moral* basis of the legal-political order with the ultimate grounding of the system of moral commitments.[61]

Each of these difficulties limited the institutionalization, on the scale of the Empire, of the underlying Roman conception of the societal community as a corporate body of citizens. By far the greatest success in overcoming the difficulties was achieved at the legal level. But, as we have mentioned, the extension of the legal status of citizenship involved a dilution of its political aspects and probably also of legal security. Important as the *jus gentium* was, it also was, in the circumstances, probably a double-edged sword.

Positively, as a universalistic normative order developed among distinct

[59] Cf. Martin P. Nilsson, *Imperial Rome* (New York: Norton Library, 1964).
[60] Ronald Syme, *The Roman Revolution* (Oxford: Clarendon Press, 1939).
[61] A. D. Nock, *Conversion* (Oxford: Oxford Paperbacks, 1961).

"ethnic" groups, the *jus gentium* was institutionalized much more thoroughly than any previous system covering a comparable range. But, negatively, the very fact that the *gens* ("people" or ethnic group) was recognized as a unit requiring legal relation to other units of its type, involved a consolidation of its inviolability. It was through membership in recognized *gentes* that individuals who were not citizens of Rome held legal rights in the Roman system—the *gens* was the external parallel to the *familia*.[62]

With this background, we may consider briefly the structure of Roman political authority. Most important was its extraordinarily unitary character. The famous formula *Senatus Populusque Romanum* (the Senate and citizenry of Rome) in certain senses carefully balanced the democratic and aristocratic principles, even though in constitutional law the senate was an organ of the people, consisting of former magistrates who, as magistrates, had been popularly elected.[63] The system became *de facto* aristocratic in that the magistrates were recruited from senatorial class lineages. However, the senators came to be drawn from increasingly broad ethnic and geographical groups, so that the senate ceased to be exclusively Roman or even Italian. Yet, the Roman state remained decidedly unitary, resting ultimately on the concept of a citizen body.[64]

Its resistance to differentiation is perhaps best illuminated by its failure to differentiate the civil executive, the military, and the judiciary as functions of "specialists." Roman magistracies carried the *imperium* (authority) of the state as a diffuse whole, having the right to exercise any aspect of the governmental powers and being differentiated only by rank.[65] Although the judicial functions were exercised by the *praetor*, he was not a lawyer, but a "politician" occupying the praetorship as a step in a public career that had probably begun with a junior military command.

The *consuls* exercised supreme military command, not in the general sense in which the American President, as Chief Executive, is also Commander-in-Chief, but in that during the Republican period, they were expected to serve as field commanders. Thus, there was no class comprised specifically of professional military officers. The case of the consulship illustrates the problems which differentiation posed for the system. Pressures to differentiate military from civil responsibility were such that frequently one *consul* acted as field commander while the other directed the civil government. Yet, that the two *consuls*, having identical legal powers, were incumbents of one category of office, not of two separate offices, shows that such pressures were sharply limited. Any differentiation was based upon informal agreement, not constitutional provision.

These facts relate to the obligation of the entire citizenry of Rome—as of most Greek *poleis*—to render military service. Indeed, as we mentioned, one may say that Rome did not "have" an army as much as it "was," in one principal aspect, an army. Perhaps it was for this reason that service in the legions

[62] Parenthetically, I suggest, the West's radical solution of this problem derived, above all, from the drastic spiritual individualism of Christianity.)

[63] H. Stuart Jones, "Administration," in Bailey (ed.), *op. cit.*

[64] Syme, *op. cit.*

[65] Jones, *op. cit.*; Nilsson, *op. cit.*

was so important a means of extending citizenship. The civil and military bases of status were very closely linked.[66]

The legislative function, insofar as it was exercised separately from other political functions, belonged most fundamentally to the "people." However, the effective institutionalization of their rights became constantly and increasingly difficult. Thus, legislation tended to center in the senate, though much of the unruliness of the city's populace and the tendency of the legions, notably the Praetorian Guard, to intervene in politics, reflected the people's lingering claim to the ultimate sovereignty. The senate became not so much a representative body as a council of elder officials having, as we stated, a *de facto* aristocratic base. Its relation to the *princeps* was inherently ambiguous and difficult,[67] a condition which was exacerbated by the principate's tendency to become hereditary *de facto*, but without firm institutionalization. Such resistance to differentiation, manifested in many contexts, is a keynote of the Roman political structure. It was a very powerful solvent for primordial solidarities, precisely because of, first, its all-or-none character and, second, the links between the unitary authority system and the legal structure of citizenship. Yet, it also tended to use political control to press the pluralistic elements of the enormously heterogeneous society into a segmentary mold. We have already alluded to this fact in the case of the early Roman family and the concentration of its rights in the status of *paterfamilias*; since the married woman could not be the legal representative of an autonomous collectivity, the tendency was to deny her all legal status. The family had to have a *potestas* (the rights to use power) as unitary as the state's *imperium*.

However, this problem was much more serious for the *gentes* of the *jus gentium*, because they were much larger units. For example, the large Jewish diaspora communities, as in Alexandria or Rome itself, were treated largely as units, being held to collective responsibilities by the state—e.g., for payment of taxes and maintenance of order among their members. Despite the many contrasts with China, there was a basic common limiting element, the failure to absorb important segments of the system into the universalistic framework. Especially outside Italy, an elaborate mosaic of unabsorbed, particularistically structured socio-cultural elements remained.[68] In this respect, though not so drastic, Roman society resembled the Islamic Empires in India—there were numerous large "Hindu" elements beneath the "Islamic" political authority.

Roman society encouraged very significant developments in public administration, trade, and the most various sorts of cultural activity. Particularly in the Antonine period, it provided political order and peace, protection of individual liberties, and economic prosperity that was unequalled, regarding both the area and population controlled and the thoroughness of control, for many centuries. The limitations we have sketched, however, probably involved not only the failure to attain modern levels of structural differentiation, but also the factors of instability which made the Western Empire, specifically, shorter-lived.

[66] Nilsson, *op. cit.*
[67] Syme, *op. cit.*, pp. 365 ff. and 407 ff.
[68] Eisenstadt, *op. cit.*

These considerations seem to link up with Weber's analysis of Rome's economic decline. Weber emphasized the system's dependence on slavery, especially for providing agricultural products on the scale required by its urban populations and wealthy classes.[69] The slave population, in turn, was recruited mainly from prisoners of war. Their organization in barracks on the *latifundia* or plantations precluded family relations and prevented the slave population from sustaining itself by natural increase. So, with the pacification of the outlying parts of the Empire, the slave supply dwindled. Family relationships had to be granted to the slaves. This led toward a semi-independent peasant agriculture and destroyed the basis of plantation production.

Certain features of the Roman political and legal system evidently constituted important factors here. In a sense, the unitary character of *imperium* was shared by the legal category of property. Something was or was not an object of possession. Hence, there was a tendency to constrict the many possible shadings of "unfreedom"—men who were not free were treated as slaves in the most drastic sense. Slavery, however, was economical only on a special basis of social organization, and when that basis was threatened, a reversion to less advanced forms ensued. Role differentiation relative to kinship and property rights was insufficient for a "formally free," individualized labor force, as Weber spoke of it.[70] The proprietary unit of a traditional kinship-based agriculture could break through to the employment of individuals only by the drastic means of categorizing "employees" as slaves. When this became untenable, a situation ensued in which security could be gained only by re-traditionalization.

It is often said that the "genius" of Rome was legal, political, and military, rather than cultural. Properly understood, this seems correct. Indeed, Roman religion was, relative to that of classical Greece, more archaic in most respects. As political rule and the legal order were extended, and the political content of citizenship attenuated, we have seen that the problem of legitimation became increasingly acute. In certain respects, during a critical period, Hellenization of the upper classes of the whole Empire, not just its Eastern half, filled the gap.[71] Perhaps the most important lasting contribution of this deveolpment was the philosophical grounding which the Stoic conception of natural law provided for the Roman legal system.

Clearly, Rome drew heavily upon the most generalized aspects of Greek classical culture in organizing the vast imperial society. Nevertheless, it lacked for a long time the capacity to develop a dynamic religious system which could legitimize and strengthen the enormously expanded societal community. The rather archaic attempt to deify the emperors was a major symptom of this—it was often treated with open ridicule by the intellectuals of the time. The need for a higher order of moral direction and legitimation was evidenced by a variegated and unstable welter of exotic cults, sects, syncretistic belief systems, and broad religious movements, many of which offered some kind of salvation to the individual. Generally, they were not, however, adequately grounded in the general culture, nor did they adequately mesh the religious needs of the

[69] Max Weber, "The Social Causes of the Decay of Ancient Civilization," in *Journal of General Education* (October, 1950).

[70] In "Sociological Categories of Economic Action," *The Theory of Social and Economic Organization, op. cit.*, Part II.

[71] Charles N. Cochrane, *Christianity and Classical Culture* (New York: Galaxy, 1957).

individual with the nature of the society as a whole, particularly in regard to the legitimation and regulation of government.[72] Like Islam, but in a somewhat different sense, Rome was overextended in these important respects. It failed to build a viable societal community, support its government, and, particularly, prevent the "alienation" of its best citizens on the requisite scale.

Sir Ernest Barker has suggested that a major reason for Christianity's eventual adoption as the state religion was a need for cultural legitimation which the previous religious culture could not provide.[73] Certainly Christianity was a religious movement with the potential to fill this need. In the early stages of its development, however, it was too other-worldly to help integrate *any* society—Gibbon's famous verdict that Christianity was a *dis*integrative force in Roman society is probably correct. Even later, it could not *simply* graft into the framework of Roman society, for the Empire involved too much that was normally alien to Christian principles. A deep societal "regression" was necessary before the religion could *grow with* the structure of a new society, before its legitimizing and regulating potential could fully develop.[74]

Conclusion

The key issue of this chapter has been the consequences of differentiating the cultural and social systems beyond the level found in archaic societies, with special reference to its implications for the nature of the societal community. In *all* four cases discussed, the patterns of the cultural system penetrated deeper into the societal structure than did *any* archaic system. Yet the cases divide into two pairs.

In China and India, the cultural system became the focus of status for well-defined upper-class groups, the scholar-gentry and the "twice-born," who collectively set the paramount tone for the society, though without corporate organization. Yet, in both cases, however differently, the societal penetration of the "cultural elites" (if this term is appropriate) was limited by a combination of their own characteristics and those of the broader societal matrices. This left a mass of undigested "primordial" populations and structures which could not, in the circumstances, be engaged in the socio-cultural patterns defined as ideal by the elite traditions in more than a lower-level sense.

Islam and Rome involved more far-reaching, "world-oriented" conceptions of societal community that were, in principle, extendable to all who could enter the cultural-social community—and neither emphasized ascriptive barriers. However, given the nature of the obstacles inherent in their social situations, and the problems of *scale* which full institutionalization of their ideal patterns would have imposed, the success of both was quite incomplete. Islam never succeeded in adequately integrating the vast *Umma* and a comparable political community. Rome failed to coordinate its broadly extended citizenship with the political, stratification, and legitimation requirements necessary for such a large body of citizens to become the effective integrative core of a viable society.

[72] See Nock, *op. cit.* and Franz Cumont, *Oriental Religions in Roman Paganism* (New York: Dover Books, 1956).

[73] Ernest Barker, "The Conception of Empire," in Bailey (ed.), *op. cit.*

[74] Cf. Ernest Troeltsch, *The Social Teachings of the Christian Churches*, Vol. I (New York: Harper Torchbooks, 1961).

Many of the most crucial ingredients of modernity were present in these societies, despite their failures to evolve into modern societies. Their primary failures were not at the level of values, but in the complex modes of integrating values with the many differentiated conditions of a complex society in a complex environment. Incapacity to cope with these conditions imposed, in turn, limits upon the development of more advanced cultural patterns. This seems particularly evident for the last two cases, which illustrate the difficulties implicit in a grand-scale "direct attack" on the problem of building a new society.

two "seed-bed" societies: Israel and Greece

six

Broadly speaking, the lower a system stands in socio-cultural evolution, the more co-extensive and less independent are its societal and cultural systems empirically. This may explain why anthropologists frequently fail to distinguish between social and cultural systems analytically and commonly speak of what we call a society as "a culture." The problem of the relation between given social and cultural systems is always complex, partly because so many components of cultural systems vary independently.

In Egypt, such co-extensiveness was clearly very tight, especially as compared with Mesopotamia. China probably exhibited the greatest degree of co-extensiveness among the "historic civilizations," though some of its culture proved exportable to Japan and other parts of East Asia, and it imported Buddhism from India. The Mediterranean world consolidated under Roman rule, on the other hand, was notably cosmopolitan in cultural terms. Yet, in the societies discussed so far, the critical effective institutionalization of cultural elements, particularly the general normative order, has occurred very predominantly within the concrete population, territory, and historical period in which the cultural developments first emerged—due allowance being made for the time processes of institutionalization take.

Buddhism is by far the most conspicuous cultural complex mentioned so far that had its most profound influence *outside* the society in which it originated. But because it did not lead toward modernity and because it had little basic significance for Western society, we have not discussed it extensively.

Two societies, though having relatively small consequence in the society-systems of their time and place, were the agents of cultural innovations that have proved of the highest significance for a wide range of societies which were not their direct evolutionary sequels—namely Israel, the originator of the religion of Jahweh (or Judaism), and Greece, the originator of a famous, largely secular culture. As the last substantive part of this small book, I would like to analyze these two cases, because they illustrate a type of contribution to the evolutionary process which has not been emphasized in previous chapters.

These cases present two primary problems. The first is to define the essential societal conditions which made their cultural innovations possible. The second is to explain how the cultural products became sufficiently dissociated from their society of origin to have such special consequences for so wide a range of subsequent societies, especially as compared to most other cultural complexes.

With respect to the first problem, we hold that these cultural innovations were so radical that their bearers could not possibly have established them over the vast territory and diverse vested interests of the large-scale "empires" of the period. The processes had to occur in small-scale societies with unusual bases of independence. In both cases, furthermore, the innovation had to involve, under the leadership of the most important classes, a differentiation of *the society as a whole* from the others to which it was closely related. It had to become a new *type of society*, not merely a new sub-system within an already existent type.[1]

With respect to the second problem, both cases had to involve a basic loss of political independence and the transfer of primary prestige within the relevant populations to elements which were not carriers of primary political responsibility at the societal level, but specialists in the maintenance and development of the distinctive cultural systems themselves.

With these considerations in mind, let us briefly review the salient facts and then attempt to formulate the factors common to both examples of this type of evolutionary process. We will not be primarily concerned with the distinctive cultural contribution of each and its specific relevance to subsequent evolution—that is reserved for the sequel book. Here our primary concern will be with the nature of the process by which such radical cultural innovations arise and are then sharply differentiated from the societal matrices of their origins.

Israel

Israel started as a tribal confederation in the fringe area between Palestine and the desert.[2] The social factors which transcended tribalism in the early period fused religious and political components in a

[1] Thus, if these two cases had a common background in the broadly New Eastern societal type of the period, as Cyrus H. Gordon has claimed in *The Common Background of Greek and Hebrew Civilizations* (New York: Norton Library, 1965), it had to be precisely a *background* that preceded the distinctive breakthroughs that each made, and *from* which each broke.

[2] Moscati, *Ancient Semitic Civilization, op. cit.*

familiar archaic manner. How far back the universalistic monotheism of Jahwism dates is controversial, but it is highly unlikely that a thorough, principled monotheism arose before the Mosaic period, and probably not even then.[3] Nevertheless, as Buber emphasizes, the characteristics of the Hebraic religion that enabled it ultimately to break through the archaic type of cultural order already had gained firm, if rudimentary, development in the Mosaic patterns of conceptualizing God and his relations with his historical people.[4]

The early Jahweh was primarily the God of the *political* confederation of Hebrews and as such was minimally implicated in the internal structure of the tribes, for which, probably, other gods long continued to be important.[5] As Weber emphasizes, Jahweh was above all the God of "foreign policy," war interests being prominent in his worship, as the appellation "Lord of Hosts" suggests.[6] During the captivity in Egypt and the conquest of the Promised Land, Jahweh was evidently not yet conceived as omnipotent, as infallibly able to guarantee his Chosen People success against any human enemies and their divine sponsors.

Israel's early social development in Palestine was broadly from a pastoral and agricultural patriarchalism to a loosely structured society of city-states. Apparently, these were quite similar to those of Mesopotamia and the Syrian-Lebanese coast, having upper classes in which member lineages were basically equal—Job seems to have been an "elder" in such a community. The lower classes were generally "clients" of the upper groups, though we should not impute too rigid a particularism to this dependency relation. Later, when monarchy emerged, Israel became a small empire not very different in basic social structure from the much larger-scale Mesopotamian type. It was, however, not especially stable nor well integrated. Although the reigns of David and Solomon consolidated the whole people of Israel into a single kingdom, it soon split into northern and southern kingdoms. In the culminating reign of Solomon, the kingdom was very much a petty "oriental monarchy" with a "national" temple cult (though in some ways a unique one), a patrician class, a patrimonial type of centralized bureaucracy, a rudimentary legal system, a semi-free peasant and artisan class, considerable market trade, a corvee for mobilizing manpower, and nomadic fringe groups who occasionally posed serious threats to political security.[7]

The most distinctive thing about the Israelites was the conception of Jahweh and the people's relation to him. This relation is grounded in the conception of the *Covenant*, which developed through several forms, most notably (for our purposes, at least) those traditionally attributed to Abraham and Moses. As Mendenhall has shown, the Covenant was conceived partly on the model of treaties between "vassal" states and "Great Kings" of dominant

[3] Theophile James Meek, *Hebrew Origins* (New York: Harper Torchbooks, 1960), Chap. 3.

[4] Martin Buber, *Moses* (New York: Harper Torchbooks, 1958).

[5] Meek, *op. cit.*

[6] Max Weber, *Ancient Judaism* (Glencoe, Ill.: The Free Press, 1952), Chap. IV.

[7] W. F. Albright, *From the Stone Age to Christianity*, 2nd ed. (Garden City: Anchor Books, 1957).

empires in the ancient Near East, particularly the Hittite Empire.[8] Thus, it subtly balanced three themes—the absolute sovereignty of God, the mutuality between God and His people, and relations among the people.

The first theme accentuates the chasm between the divine and the human which marks their more generalized differentiation. However much later development there was, this theme is the point of entrance for the concept of a transcendent God that eventually made His attributes inconceivable in human terms. Thus, His plans and will were not to be evaluated by human needs or standards. Although "staying on the right side" of Jahweh in the sense of propitiation was important (indeed essential), more crucial was the conception that His people lived to do His will as a collectivity. This belief is the substance of the very important shift in relations with the divine, from religious "bartering" with it—typical of archaic religions—to serving as *its instrument*.[9] Among the main themes of Egyptian religion outlined by Frankfort, creation took clear precedence for Israel, while procreation and resurrection (in Frankfort's sense) receded to virtual insignificance. The Chosen People were, by God's creative act, endowed with a divine *mission*, a conception involving a major step beyond, not merely the Egyptian, but also the Mesopotamian belief system.

Thus, no Israelitic King could legitimately claim any semblance of divinity within the bounds of strict Hebrew religion. He was merely the human leader of a human community which took its mandate from God, but in no way "participated" in the divine. Indeed, it seems that a tendency of Solomon to claim some sort of divine status was a major factor in the Prophets' opposition to the monarchy.[10] At any rate, the main trend of Israelitic thought clearly established a gulf between the divine and the human that was as radically unbridgeable for the higher human echelons as for the lower ones. This certainly relates to the fact that a special prestige status was never firmly institutionalized for the Israelitic priesthood. The king having *no* godhead himself, had no special priestly charisma, quite unlike his Mesopotamian and, particularly, his Egyptian counterparts.

Indeed the Covenant had profound significance for the organizational development of religious action. A primary religious focus on cult was characteristic of archaic civilizations. This was by no means absent in Israel, but the developmental trend of religion based on the Covenant was to ethical instruction and, above all, to law.

In early times, Jahweh's sacrificial cult was practiced by all important dignitaries, particularly the "patriarchs," heads of lineage groups.[11] Eventually, however, the cult, which (following the terms of the Covenant) came to mediate between God and the people of Israel collectively, was centralized in the great temple at Jerusalem and practiced by its special priesthood. Numerous cultist elements did remain scattered about the countryside, but they were generally diffusely embedded in other statuses, mostly of intra-tribal significance, and often were independent of Jahweh worship or, like the

[8] George E. Mendenhall, *Law and Covenant in Israel and the Ancient Near East* (Pittsburgh: Biblical Colloquium, 1959).
[9] Weber, *Ancient Judaism, op. cit.*
[10] Frankfort, *Kingship and the Gods, op. cit.*, concluding chap., "The Hebrews."
[11] Meek, *op. cit.*, Chap. 4.

Baal cults, were even opposed to it and curtailed by it.[12] Thus, Israel lacked extensive priesthoods constituting a structurally distinct, high-status sector of the society, as in Egypt or Mesopotamia. As Weber emphasized, this feature of the society resulted in an interest structure relatively open to anti-traditionalist influences.

During the period of political independence, the sacrificial cult came to be centered in the temple at Jerusalem and was effectively eliminated from the constituent units, such as lineages and local communities. Yet, Solomon's temple, as the central symbol of Israel, was an archaic element. The experience of having to live in the Diaspora without a temple cult—particularly during the Babylonian captivity—prepared the way for the later form of Judaism. This emerged after the destruction of the temple, when the cult element disappeared entirely, but without destroying the ethnic and cultural identity of the people of Israel.

Concurrently with this de-emphasis on cult, Judaism developed a second characteristic for which, besides its transcendental theism, it is highly distinctive, namely the belief in the special significance of the law as distinct from the cult. This emphasis, which probably emerged clearly only after Moses, followed from the belief that the primary religious obligation was less to worship Jahweh than to *obey* him. The law, traditionally grounded in the Mosaic Decalogue, became increasingly the charter of the people. Their common acceptance of it and, through that, their special relation to its divine author constituted their identity as an ethnic community.[13] We have pointed out that very important legal developments had occurred in Mesopotamia. Except for specifically religious items, such as the First Commandment, the Israelitic law was not fundamentally different in content from such developments, although it did tend to eliminate class differences in legal rights and obligations.[14] Its unique quality lay in the *meaning* attributed to it. Not simply the king's exercise of authority over relations among his subjects or between his regime and his subjects, it constituted the *content* of God's will for his people. It was Jahweh's "Commandments."

Therefore, whatever the human organization of political authority, the fundamental normative order governing human relations was to be considered *independent* of it. The king, insofar as the kingdom was Israelitic, was to act *under* the law and be the agent of its implementation, not its source and origin. Under non-Israelitic rule, the Jew's first obligation was to the Jewish law, not to the political authority [15]—this is the point of the episode involving Daniel and his associates in Babylon. The religious and secular components of this normative order were not yet differentiated, and both aspects of the developing law were highly particularized in substance. Indeed, they became continually more so in post-exilic times.[16] Further advances occurred only much later, under exceedingly different conditions.

Despite legitimizing the law of the community on religious grounds, the

[12] *Ibid.*; Weber, *Ancient Judaism, op. cit.*, Chaps. VI and VIII.

[13] *Ibid.*

[14] Moscati, *Ancient Semitic Civilization, op. cit.*; Albright, *op. cit.*

[15] Martin Buber, *The Prophetic Faith* (New York: Harper Torchbooks, 1960), *passim.*

[16] Rudolph Bultmann, *Primitive Christianity in its Contemporary Setting* (Cleveland: Meridian Books, 1956), pp. 59 ff.

Israelitic system strongly maintained its direct relevance to practical human affairs. The transcendence of the source of legitimation did not imply that only other-worldly action could be accorded high religious merit, as Indian doctrine tended to hold. Jahweh's will for his people profoundly involved their proper management, as a social community, of this-worldly, even ordinary, affairs.

The status of the law as the means of relating to Jahweh provided the most important grounding for the special nature of the Israelitic societal community, usually designated as the *people*. The people were defined both by having been "chosen" and by having (in some sense) voluntarily associated themselves. Thus, mutual commitment, both to Jahweh and to one another, defined their solidarity.

First, this conception of the "people" provided the constitutive symbolism for maintaining the societal identity which survived, not so much "persecution", as the absorbent pressures of complex societies organized on a much larger scale than Israel. The stories of Joseph and Potiphar's wife and Daniel in Babylon illustrate the importance of this communal identity.

Second, this identity was the basis of an internal leveling tendency. As we mentioned, the Kingdom of Solomon was rigidly stratified according to the pattern of the times. As Israel's special nature and status became more salient, however, greater pressure developed to define all Hebrews as having the same problem.[17] Hence, the distinction between belonging and not belonging became emphasized, rather than differentiations within the community of Israel itself. Third, the *basis* of commitment, not only (as in Job's case) toward Jahweh, but also toward the community of Israel, became particularly troublesome and had to be resolved fundamentally on *voluntary* grounds. Adjacent societies offered numerous and attractive opportunities for defection from the community.

There seems to be no doubt that the central focus of Judaism was the conception of the people as the societal community which bore the distinctive culture. However, the leveling tendency and the note of voluntary adherence also developed important seeds of religious individualism, which became more prominent in later periods and fed into the stream of Christian individualism.[18]

The covenant relation thus motivated positive loyalties to the religion of Jahweh and to the community of the people, without converting the Hebrews into a band of special, fissive devotees or a small ascetic or sectarian order that could not involve a whole ethnic community.

Although Jahweh's transcendence so surpassed humanity that a human contract could not bind Him, essential to the Covenant were His favorable promises to the people, contingent, most conspicuously in the Mosaic Covenant, on their fulfillment of His Commandments.[19] Faith in Jahweh, then, could not very well be expressed if His conduct were conceived as totally arbitrary—i.e., if divine promises were not "morally binding," so that the man or community who lived faithfully according to the law could have no legitimate

[17] Weber, *Ancient Judaism, op. cit.*, Part IV; and Buber, *The Prophetic Faith, op cit.*

[18] Bultmann, *op. cit.;* Eric Voegelin, *Israel and Revelation*, vol. I of *Order and History* (New Orleans: Louisiana State University Press, 1956), Chap. 13, especially Part 3.

[19] Weber, *Ancient Judaism, op. cit.*, Chap. V, IX, XII.

complaints if punishment rather than reward resulted. This was the problem that the Book of Job brought into sharp focus. Also common was a complementary expectation that an individual's "seed" would be rewarded for his faith if he were not. But however many such formulations are possible, some expectation of reward is required to ground faith as a crucial medium for motivating people to higher achievements. Thus, a Covenant by which Israel was "chosen," but which left Jahweh morally free to treat His people as He saw fit, regardless of their behavior, could not have been sufficiently meaningful in terms of this orientation, however prominent it has been since, as in the theology of Augustine and the early Church Reformers, for example. Equally essential, however, was the concept that the Jew was not to count upon *immediate* reward.

Until the Prophetic Age, Judaism was bound to a politically independent community which stood in a peculiarly precarious position between the great powers, Egypt and Babylonia.[20] Not only small and weak, it easily appeared arrogant and pretentious, claiming to be the Chosen People of a supreme god, if not *the* supreme God. It would seem that, on such a basis, the only alternative to probable extinction was the course later taken by Islam—expansion and absorption of its neighbors. This was simply not a realistic possibility in the circumstances. But however that may be, Israel took a very different course, through the Prophetic movement.

Basically, this course was the renouncement of the *right* to political autonomy: the Babylonian conquest was accepted as not only inevitable, but as somehow legitimate—a punishment handed down by God on his people for their failure to keep His Commandments. Although very much a reaction against the monarchy and the upper classes, the Prophetic movement did not attempt to take over from them, as is normal for "revolutionary" movements, but rather to deflect the line of social development in a basically different direction.[21] It projected fulfillment in a "land of milk and honey" into an indefinite future, accepting a correspondingly indefinite period of penitent purification in the Diaspora state.

Thus, whatever the respective contributions of internal tensions and feelings of injustice and threats of invasion from Mesopotamia, the Prophetic movement tended to shift the central problem of meaning from here and now rewards to the eventual fate of Israel. This involved both drastically deflating optimism about the present and the immediate future and interpreting the unfavorable situation in terms of the people's guilt for not having kept Jahweh's Commandments. Bringing Babylonia into the system, however, made it necessary to accentuate, if not originate, the conception that Jahweh was not just the Israelites' God, but *the* universal God, who could manifest His will and power by using the Babylonians to chastise His people for their sins.[22]

Through processes related to these developments, Israelitic culture attained a new level of literacy. The basic reference for the community's constitution was its Covenant relation with Jahweh. The very meaning of this relation

[20] *Ibid.*
[21] *Ibid.*; also, cf. Buber, *The Prophetic Faith*, *op. cit.*
[22] Voegelin, *op. cit.*; Weber, *Ancient Judaism*, *op. cit.*, Chap. XII.

was increasingly to be found in the content of the God-given law. This placed a tremendous premium on knowledge of the law, which, in turn, required emphasizing its authoritative documentation. Israel, thus, became preeminently a people of the Book.[23]

As we have mentioned, in early times sacrificial rites were apparently quite prominent, the Levite tribe even claiming ascriptive control over correct sacrificial ritual, though in the patriarchal period they did not themselves officiate as priests—this role was performed by the patriarchal lineage heads.[24] They acted analogously to the parliamentarian of a convention, being expert on correct procedure. It was, however, difficult to draw a clear line between such ritual concerns and the elements of law regulating ordinary social relationships. A special premium was then placed on knowledge of the law in general, not only its specifically ritual elements, and it became impossible for any particular group to monopolize relevant legal knowledge.

Generally, then, this function was universalized—e.g., in the hands of the Rabbinate and the Pharisees, learning in the law eventually became independent of ascribed positions or special offices.[25] Moreover, there was a strong emphasis on having *all* the more responsible community members share a basic legal competence. This obviously depended on their being literate and able to discuss relevant problems with the rabbis or Pharisees. We can thus regard Israel as among the first societies to develop a fully literate upper class, practically all of whose male adult members were schooled in the basic religious documents.

Despite the particularism of the Chosen People concept, Israel, as a societal community, regulated itself and defined its identity according to a normative order which was divinely bestowed, not its own internal matter. This order was objectively contained in canonical documents, knowledge of which grounded the legitimacy of the main patterns of human relations, including political authority. Furthermore, the belief that Jahweh was *the* universal God, not merely Israel's God, meant that, in some sense, his normative order should be applicable to *all* mankind.

This resulted in the conception of a moral order governing human affairs that, being controlled by a transcendental God, was independent of *any* particular societal or political organization. Jahweh could punish indigenous kings and use nonbelieving emperors as his instruments. Such beliefs sustained the dispersed Jewish community when it lost political independence, through the gradual realization that this loss was permanent, and even after the sacrificial cult was extinguished by the Temple's destruction.[26] This peculiar cultural complex: first a transcendental "legislator" god; second, a moral order prescribed by him; and third, the idea of a holy community executing his mandate, was able not only to survive the ending of a politically independent Israel, but eventually to become independent of the Israelitic community's dispersed units and be transferred to non-Israelitic societies and collectivities. This, I believe, was Israel's great contribution to social evolution.[27]

[23] *Ibid.*, especially Chaps. III, XII, and XV.
[24] Meek, *op. cit.*, Chap. IV.
[25] Bultmann, *op. cit.*
[26] *Ibid.*, p. 80 ff.
[27] Weber, *Ancient Judaism, op. cit.*, Chaps. XIV and XV.

Greece

The social and cultural continuities among ancient Near Eastern societies have, until very recently, generally been greatly underestimated. Available evidence indicates that there was a basic continuity in "city-state" structure from Mesopotamia to the Greek mainland and islands, including Cyprus, Crete, and the Syrian and Aegean shores of Asia.[28] In this respect, the "Dorian invasion" of Greece apparently introduced a less drastic break than was long believed.

Unlike Israel, however, the Greek city-states were the only "more civilized" small units, aside from certain Phoenician communities, which typically maintained their political independence.[29]

Although Israel was very small in comparison with the great archaic empires, it was nevertheless a monarchical consolidation of many "tribes" and, later, of city-states which probably cross-cut them. *This* consolidated nation defined and bore the distinctive cultural pattern, Jahweh's religion, and the law he prescribed. The unit of the people, though small by empire standards, far transcended the city-state.

Whereas the tiny *polis* was the primary societal unit, the major Greek *cultural* pattern coalesced about the language and certain written forms of heritage involved in it, particularly, among the early documents, the poems of Homer and Hesiod.[30] This linguistic-literary culture—varied and diffuse—was borne by many politically independent *poleis* which, during the classical period, were restricted primarily to the city-state level of organization. The combination and interaction of such a single common culture with such a multiplicity of societal units certainly contributed a great deal to the special creativity of Greek civilization.

The uniformity among the Greek city-states, on the basis just outlined, was thus *primarily cultural,* although it also included such politically relevant elements as strong feelings for the distinction between Greeks and barbarians. Beyond that, however, it also involved very considerable interaction. Though Greeks fought Greeks in continual inter-polis warfare, there also was much friendly and meaningful visiting, official and unofficial. There were elaborate diplomatic relations and alliances against outsiders, particularly against Persia during the great crisis of the early fifth century. Certain "international" institutions, particularly the Oracle and Shrine of Delphi and the centers at Olympia and Epidaurus, were also important. At these sites, masses assembled from the entire Greek world on varieties of errands and occasions.[31] Each of the centers concerned the religious culture common to all Greeks, but had its special emphasis. Delphi, which commanded the greatest dignity, was religio-political in focus—in a sense the "United Nations" of the Greek world. Olympia

[28] See, for example, Gordon, *op. cit.;* Olmstead, *op cit.;* Eric Voegelin, *The World of the Polis* (New Orleans: Louisiana State University Press, 1957), especially Chap. I; Donald Hardin, *The Phoenicians* (New York: Praeger Paperbacks, 1962); and Martin P. Nilsson, *Minoan-Mycenean Religion and its Survival in Greek Religion,* 2nd ed. (Lund: Gleering, 1950).

[29] Victor Ehrenberg, *The Greek State* (New York: Norton, 1964), Chap. I.

[30] See especially, Werner Jaeger, *Paideia: The Ideals of Greek Culture,* Vol. I (New York: Oxford University Press, 1945), Book One, Chap. III, "Homer the Educator."

[31] Martin P. Nilsson, *Greek Folk Religion* (New York: Harper Torchbooks, 1961).

was oriented more to the important cult of physical fitness and beauty, and Epidaurus more to that of health.[32]

The religion which grounded this Greek "international" order was notably polytheistic and, hence, in a sense, pluralistic, specifically in contrast to Judaism, which emphasized the whole community's relation to *one* God and his unitary will for their role in His creation. Nevertheless, the consequences of the Greek and Israelitic patterns converged in one crucial respect. Because it was pan-Hellenic, Greek culture, like Israelitic culture, transcended any single politically organized community. In Greece as in Israel, no king or, later, assembly of citizens, whether constituted aristocratically or democratically, could claim "sovereignty" in the sense in which it was claimed in Egypt, or even in Mesopotamia, in the sense that *this* actual polity could be identified with the ultimate source of universal order.[33] The Israelites had a transcendent normative authority, the will of Jahweh, to which they had to *adapt*. The Greeks conceived such authority not as the will of any particular deity but as an order divinely existent and imposed upon them, that eventually came to be formulated as the order of nature. This was independent of the politically organized community in a sense totally unknown to archaic societies. Indeed, it bound the gods, themselves.[34]

Almost certainly, this more general conception of order was an essential condition of the distinctive Greek pattern of social organization. It carried the basic equality of the city-state's constituent elements farther than any previous cultural pattern. The earliest Greek *polis* structure was evidently rather continuous with the general city-state pattern of the Near East, including Mesopotamia. In each case, it was formed by a religiously grounded confederation of lineages which constituted the upper class of a two-class system.[35] The male heads of the upper-class lineages were formally equal. The kings of the pre-classical period, like Agamemnon, Menelaus, or Priam in the *Iliad*, were certainly considered first among equals.[36] Furthermore, under Greek conditions, such a king could never obtain by conquest the paramount positions in other city-states, as Mesopotamian kings commonly did.

Although even classical Greece was divided into aristocratic-oligarchic and democratic *poleis*, the principle that the *polis* was a corporate group of citizens within which formal equality should prevail in regard to basic citizenship rights, including some participation in government, was central to all.[37] Even oligarchs and "tyrants" were, in an important sense, "spokesmen" for the community of citizens; indeed, the "tyrants" played crucial roles in democratizing certain *poleis*. On the basis of this corporate principle, a num-

[32] As a psychiatrist told me after a visit there, "perhaps the best mental hospital of historic times."

[33] Voegelin, *The World of the Polis*, *op. cit.*, especially his discussion of the *Iliad*, which shows how the actions of even heroes and gods were transcended by principles of the normative order.

[34] *Ibid.*, *passim*.

[35] Martin P. Nilsson, *A History of Greek Religion* (Oxford: Clarendon Press, 1949), Chap. VII, especially pp. 244–249.

[36] W. Warde Fowler, *The City-State of the Greeks and Romans* (London: Macmillan, 1921), Chap. II.

[37] Ehrenberg, *op. cit.*, Chap. II, especially Part V.

ber of *poleis,* most notably Athens, developed full democracy for the male citizenry, with equality of the franchise and other basic rights before the law, including rights in litigation before a "jury" of peers.[38] To be sure, such democracy often approached benevolent dictatorship in order to maintain its cohesiveness and effectiveness, as occurred in Athens under Pericles; but this does not diminish the great significance of the achievement.

In line with the general characteristics of "historic" intermediate societies, this relatively egalitarian corporate community, the citizen body, comprised an upper class within a larger system, much of which was denied full rights of membership. Strikingly, the citizens of the *polis* were normally a minority. It is estimated that the Athens of the Periclean Age had only about 30,000 citizens, including women and children, in a total population of about 150,000. The remainder were slaves and "metics," resident aliens, some of whose ancestors had been "resident" for many generations. Complete inclusion in a societal community on a full-membership, democratic basis had to await early modern types of society, though in one aspect it was, as we have seen, developed in Rome.[39] Outside the territorial limits of the entire Greek political system, as well as of the particular *polis,* were the "barbarians," who were quite definitely "lower class" in terms of cultural value.

Because, as an upper class, it devoted so much of its time primarily to government and war, the citizen group, or much of it, was economically dependent on these subordinated groups, even under such simple economic conditions. Moreover, the *poleis* had to be very simple governmentally, above all not requiring much bureaucratization because safeguards preserving the interests of the citizens greatly encumbered administration, both civil and military.[40] Indeed, Sparta, in specializing as a military *polis,* became a principal agency in the system's disintegration, for loosely organized Athens could not compete over the long run with its military efficiency.

Internal *stasis,* or class conflict, and inter-*polis* warfare were the most immediate factors that destroyed the *polis* system.[41] It was highly vulnerable to intervention by an outside expansionist power, squeaking by the threat of Persia very narrowly and, only a century later, succumbing to Macedonia. Its independence during the highly creative phase was very short.

Let us consider again the principal developments of the Greek cultural pattern. In a certain sense, its religious grounding was obverse to Israel's. The latter exalted divinity far above the level of archaic polytheism and gave it transcendence, unity, and coherence, so that the human level, being sharply differentiated from the divine, was thereby endowed with its own special independence and, indeed, dignity. The Greeks, on the other hand, humanized the gods, even attributing to them many ordinary human failings, such as

[38] C. Hignett, *A History of the Athenian Constitution* (Oxford: Clarendon Press, 1952).

[39] Internally, the Jewish Diaspora community probably came closer to the concept of full inclusion than any Greek *polis*. However, it was clearly not a society, but an "ethnic" enclave within a "host" society. The "Gentiles," although they were the power-holding majority of the host society, were, from the Jewish point of view, the disqualified "lower class." Elaborate ritual measures maintaining separateness from the Gentiles were a very salient feature of post-exilic Judaism. Cf. Weber, *Ancient Judaism, op. cit.*

[40] W. C. Beyer, "The Civil Service of the Ancient World" in *Public Administration Review* (1959) 19:243–249.

[41] Olmstead, *op. cit.;* Ehrenberg, *op. cit.*

vanity and jealousy. However, they conceived both gods and men as subject to a binding order of nature which, in the first instance, was normative. This conception of order, itself, underwent very important development and generalization.

Significant here is the juxtaposition common in all classical thought, particularly its drama, between an archaic and a more advanced conception of order.[42] For example, in the Oedipus trilogy of Sophocles, the fundamental conception concerns the absolutely ineluctable consequences of the normative order with respect to the problem of incest. The pathos in Oedipus' situation regarding his inescapable fate is surely comparable to that of Job's (and that of Calvinistic predestination). And, as with Job, intentional motivation to violate the order is ruled out: Oedipus could not possibly have known that he had killed his father and married his mother. Nevertheless, the consequences of infraction inexorably follow these acts, regardless of their motivation.

Sophocles then generalizes this inexorable order to a new normative level through the intervention of Theseus, who symbolizes Athenian civilization. In death (significantly) Oedipus is absolved from his "sins," apotheosized as basically guiltless, and admitted to the holy fraternity of Athenian citizenship. It seems that Sophocles was saying that the *polis*' kinship-incest based archaic order had been superseded by an order based on "civic" relationship.[43] The latter, we may say, became altogether dissociated from the kinship aspects of the normative order except, in the Athenian case, for citizenship eligibility, which remained closely ascribed to kinship—but even this was symbolically broken through in Oedipus' case.

Similar themes were formulated even more sharply by the philosophers. Socrates' basic polemic against the Sophists concerned their relativism. He asserted the ultimate propriety of a civil justice which both transcended the Sophistic relativisms—e.g., the "right of the stronger"—and rejected the traditional norms from which the Sophists had emancipated Greek thought.[44] The justice of Socrates and Plato was grounded in a universalistic conception of general order. This order, accessible to understanding through reason, was superior—in conceptual generalization and in the potential for social development that could be realized from its institutionalization—to both morally nihilistic acceptance of civic struggle (as propounded by Thrasymachus) and the archaic traditionalism of the type that plagued Oedipus with ascriptive obligations and admitted the meaningfulness of whimsical acts from the gods.[45] It was the first formal and general conceptualization of the normative framework of human life which clearly abstracted moral obligations from the nonhuman elements, including the divine, involved in the condition of action. It was later reformulated by the Stoics as the Law of Nature.

As the political thought of Plato and Aristotle clearly shows, the universalistic potential of the Natural Order concept was not institutionalized in the political organization of the time. Indeed, both philosophers believed the small *poleis* to be the only ethically acceptable political organizations,

[42] Voegelin, *The World of the Polis, op. cit.*; E. R. Dodds, *The Greeks and the Irrational* (Boston: Beacon Paperbacks, 1957).
[43] Kenneth Burke, *Poetics* (unpublished manuscript).
[44] Jaeger, *op. cit.*, Book I, Chap. 9; Book II, Chap. III.
[45] Jaeger, *Paideia: The Ideals of Greek Culture*, Vol. II, *passim*.

all larger-scale polities being barbaric in form. Yet, Aristotle's private thoughts on the political goals of his employer, Philip, and his pupil, Alexander, would be interesting, as it seems very unlikely that he could consider their visions of a large-scale polity as simply barbarous.

Greece, then, like the people of Israel, developed a highly distinctive cultural system by a process which involved the radical differentiation of the *whole* societal unit from other societal types. Most important, the *polis* developed into a *corporate* body of citizens which became (especially in the leading, exemplary case of Athens) a body of equals, though non-citizen residents were excluded and remained a "lower class." During this development, the Greek world enjoyed a precarious freedom from intervention by great powers. This condition not only encouraged fragmentation, but also continual internecine wars. Such radical autonomy on the part of the individual *poleis* was probably an *essential* condition for the development of their highly special social and cultural patterns. Largely because of it, however, Greece was nearly conquered by Persia, and actually succumbed to Macedonia a century later.[46]

The Greek development was somewhat more complicated than Israel's in that its cultural complex was borne through the critical period of its emergence by a considerable number of very small independent societal units. The cultural preeminence of Athens, however, certainly gave coherence to the movement, especially since Athens attracted talent from all over the Greek world.

The process by which Greek culture was separated from its original cultural matrix was precipitated by the Macedonian conquest, after which the Greek *poleis* never regained their political independence. Yet the process was somewhat different form the Israelitic case. Philip and Alexander were marginal Greeks, and the Hellenistic kingdoms made Greek the language of their courts and, eventually, of their educated classes generally. Thus, for example, the Septuagint (the translation of the Old Testament into Greek) was occasioned because the educated Jews of Alexandria read Greek more generally than Hebrew. Greek culture, then, became paramount throughout the whole eastern Mediterranean region and extended quite far into the East. Basically, its eminence continued throughout the Roman period. It was, of course, spread rather thinly over the welter of other traditions in the area, which were never, as we have noted, very fully absorbed into the Roman community. But, until the rise of Christianity, there was no broad cultural tradition which could strongly compete with Greek "philosophy" for the interest and allegiance of the intellectual elite.[47] Hence, it was in a strategic position to exert a massive impact on any process of cultural innovation occurring in that area. In fact, it became one of the primary constituents of the Christian movement, particularly through the influence of the Alexandrian school of theology.[48]

[46] Max Weber, in a famous exchange with the ancient historian Eduard Meyer, argued that a Persian victory at Marathon or Salamis would have changed the whole course of Western history. Almost certainly, it would have cut short the development of Greek secular culture, which then could not have become a major constituent in, respectively, Hellenistic, Roman, and modern Western society. (Cf. Max Weber, *Gesammelte Aufsatze zur Sozial- und Wirtschaftsgeschichte* (Tubingen: J. C. B. Mohr, 1924), Chap. I, sections 4 and 5.

[47] A. D. Nock, *Conversion, op. cit.*

[48] Werner Jaeger, *Early Christianity and Greek Paideia* (Cambridge: Harvard University Press, 1961).

Of course, the mobility and individualism of the Hellenistic and Roman societies were essential conditions of this influence.

From the Macedonian era, however, the societal bearer of Greek culture was no longer the individual *polis* or system of *poleis*. To be sure, Athens retained its high intellectual prestige throughout the whole Roman period. For example, it was fashionable for Roman aristocratic families to send their sons to Athens for a kind of "finishing" education; and Greek teachers, many trained in Athens, were an important intellectual influence throughout the Empire. Gradually, however, the intellectual center of gravity moved to Alexandria, which, for example, was the center of the development of Greek science in which Euclid and Ptolemy were so prominent.

Thus, although there was no Greek Diaspora, certain essential conditions were equivalent. Emerging from both Jewish and Greek culture were scholar classes—the rabbis and philosophers—that did not command the same order of political status and responsibility that had been carried by pre-Exile Hebrews and fifth-century Greeks. Their social status in their respective communities became the principal societal anchorages of their relatively independent cultural traditions.

seven

conclusion

Although the conception of societal evolution has probably been this book's dominant perspective, it is not just a neo-evolutionary essay which claims that the old social evolutionists were simply right after all. Rather, it belongs to a movement in contemporary social science which aspires to emulate the much grander Renaissance by doing more than merely reviving old ideas. Thus, we have reconsidered the idea of social evolution in the context of the major theoretical and empirical advances that have accumulated since the earlier evolutionists wrote.

If the latter were right that the idea is fruitful (I would call it essential), the progress of social science in the last two generations has certainly made it enormously more fruitful. Furthermore, this progress fits into certain more general developments in modern science. Advances in the biological sciences since, for example, Herbert Spencer's day, have generated altogether new conceptions of the fundamental continuity between general organic evolution and sociocultural evolution.[1] Because early evolutionary theory treated society and culture largely by imputing causation to environmental factors[2] within the old dichotomous framework of, not just heredity *and* environment, but actually heredity *versus* environment, it necessarily conceived of organic and "cultural" evolution as radically discontinuous. This perspective provided important grounding for early anthropology and other currents in social thought flowing partly from idealist sources. However, the discontinuity it hypothesized is no longer justifiable in the context of modern biology.

To be an evolutionist, one must define a general trend in evolution—

[1] See Sol Tax (ed.), *Evolution after Darwin*, 3 Vols.; especially Vol. II, *The Evolution of Man* (Chicago: The University of Chicago Press, 1960).

[2] In this case, both physical and cultural.

one cannot be a radical cultural relativist who regards the Arunta of Australia and such modern societies as the Soviet Union as equally authentic "cultures," to be judged as equals in *all basic* respects. Our perspective clearly involves evolutionary judgments—for example, that intermediate societies are more advanced than primitive societies, and modern societies, though not discussed in this volume, are more advanced than intermediate societies. I have tried to make my basic criterion congruent with that used in biological theory, calling more "advanced" the systems that display greater generalized adaptive capacity.

The present analysis differs significantly from most older evolutionary theories in that the developmental dimension I have used is fully compatible with the idea that there is considerable variability and branching among lines of evolution. The evidence we have reviewed indicates that, in the earlier stages of evolution, there have been *multiple* and *variable* origins of the *basic* societal types. Thus, we need not postulate one primitive origin of all intermediate societies, even though we consider such factors as independent cultural legitimation and stratification *necessary* conditions of all intermediate societies. At all stages, the importance of such variability can be adequately treated, we argue, only by an analytic theory of variable factors and components. The impressive development of such theory since Spencer's time enables us to construct a much more sophisticated evolutionary scheme than his.

Crucially, there are two types of societies besides those which historical evidence links through continuous processes to evolutionary advancement. First are those which have been eliminated by the socio-cultural version of the negative aspect of natural selection—e.g., no close approximation of ancient Israel or Greece has survived as a society in the modern world. Yet, the fact that the Kingdom of David and Solomon and the *polis* of Athens were eliminated did not, we have argued, destroy their future *cultural* contribution. Second are those which, though not developing into more advanced types, are established in "niches" which, despite the existence of more advanced societies, permit them to survive for long periods of time without undergoing basic changes of pattern. The many primitive societies studied by anthropologists are of this type. Quite clearly, we must postulate that their characteristics significantly approximate those of our own actual pre-historical antecedents. The exact extent of such approximation, however, can be determined only by technical procedures which are still very imprecise and imperfect.

Condensing our very broad analysis into such limited space has created a distinct bias. In dealing with the main patterns of evolutionary development, we have focused on the societies and structural components which gave rise to the most important developments. It has not been possible within the present limits to give equal attention to either of the above two types of "dead-end" cases, though Israel and Greece have been surveyed from the standpoint of their cultural developments. I have tried to be conscientious on this point by emphasizing the *failure* of adaptive development in a number of societal cases. However, an adequate treatment of the empirical *balance* of successes and failures, and the factors determining them, would require a different order of study.[3]

[3] The problem of failures is treated much more fully in S. N. Eisenstadt, *The Political Systems of Empires* (New York: The Free Press of Glencoe, 1963), and a number of Eisenstadt's recent papers, some of which are included in his *Essays in Comparative Institutions* (New York: Wiley, 1965).

In this discussion, one crucial difference between socio-cultural evolution and organic evolution must be kept in mind: Cultural patterns and content can be *diffused,* not only from generation to generation within a society, but also from society to society. This point becomes crucial when considering cases like Israel and Greece.

Regarding methods of study, there is another exceedingly important parallel, or continuity, between organic and socio-cultural evolution: Structural analysis must take a certain priority over the analysis of process and change. This may not hold for all social science, but its validity for the subject of this book can hardly be doubted. One need not develop a truly advanced general analysis of the main *processes* of social change in order to make general claims about the *structural patterning* of evolutionary development. This fact is well established in biology, where morphology, including comparative anatomy, is the "backbone" of evolutionary theory. Although Darwin advanced crucial ideas about process in the principle of natural selection, he stated explicitly that he could not prove in even a single case that it has changed one species into another, but only that "it groups and explains well a host of facts . . .", the vast majority of which concerned structure.[4] Darwin simply did not present a developed "theory of evolutionary process," especially in regard to the genesis of variations. But this did not impugn the entire scientific status of the theory of organic evolution as Darwin developed it.

It is necessary to stress this point because some sociologists insist that only "dynamic" analysis has any scientific standing. Emphatically, I am not saying that contributions to the analysis of process and change would not improve evolutionary theory enormously. But I am saying that the use of available sociological, anthropological, archaeological, and historical evidence to order structural types and relate them sequentially is a *first* order of business which cannot be by-passed. Furthermore, the task is as much theoretical as empirical, for reasons which should be very clear by now.

If such advanced structural knowledge is to be developed and utilized, social science must do a great deal of theoretical work, as well as continuing empirical research. Certainly Max Weber's extensive system of ideal types far surpassed, some half century ago, all earlier structural analysis. Furthermore, Weber's formulations were most intimately associated with great ranges of historical and comparative material, mastered extraordinarily well. Particularly noteworthy is that, notwithstanding Weber's special concern with religion and cultural movements, much of his structural theory concerned economic and political organization.[5]

The present generation of sociologists is making the first major advances on Weber's work in these fields. In the area of theory, there has now been sufficient advance so that most of the difficulties of Weber's "type atomism"

[4] Charles Darwin, quoted in the "Preface" to Talcott Parsons, Edward A. Shils, Kasper D. Naegele, and Jesse R. Pitts (eds.), *Theories of Society* (New York: The Free Press of Glencoe, 1961).

[5] Cf. Talcott Parsons, "Value Objectivity in Social Science: an Interpretation of Max Weber's Contribution," Max Weber Centennial article in *International Social Science Journal* (1965) 27:No. 1.

can be avoided. To a much greater degree, variability can now be analyzed as a function of different combinations of the same analytically defined components.[6]

Since we have ended the present volume with the advanced intermediate societies, it has been necessary to rely primarily on the more "humanistic" traditions of historical, archaeological, and anthropological research. Their methods have been improved greatly in the last two generations. For example, our account of Egyptian society would not have been possible had we based it on the Egyptology of Breasted's era (the early decades of this century). The most important advances in quantitative social science research are much more relevant in dealing with the subject of the subsequent volume, modern societies. However, there is one important context in which they are highly relevant for further study of the subject matter of this book. That is, among contemporaneous societies, we can find approximations of many of the major societal types involved in the evolutionary sequence we have discussed. The development of the comparative method is being extended to include a variety of underdeveloped societies as well as the most advanced modern types. Although it was tempting to mobilize such material for our purposes, the difficulties of interrelating it with the historical data concerned with the main flourishing of intermediate societies would have been both empirically and theoretically formidable—probably impossible within the stringent space limits of this book, unless we had given up our more historical analysis. Since a choice was inevitable, it seemed logical for an evolutionary study to follow a more temporally ordered framework, with the necessary exception of contemporary primitive societies, for which no direct historical data exist.

Comparative study is also stimulating a new level of interdisciplinary research. Here two major shifts have emerged. First, anthropology, with its predilection for studying small-scale societies largely without recent, more technical methods, has become *relatively* less prominent. The more comparative work, especially on "development," has been done primarily by economists, political scientists, and sociologists. This move has greatly advanced the integration of comparative studies and the larger corpus of social science, a factor now affecting both very significantly. Second, inter-disciplinary collaboration in the social sciences, which during and after World War II concentrated largely on "Area Studies" of particular national societies and regional complexes, is now shifting toward a more explicitly comparative perspective. Concomitantly, there has been growing concern with generalization, both theoretical and empirical. These statements are particularly true of American social science.

Only against this background is the present kind of essay understandable. It attempts a very general structural analysis and a more limited processual one. But, in formulating and validating its propositions, it has also attempted to use the best available empirical materials.

Clearly, the structural ordering of social data, essential as it is, should never be too much dissociated from the analysis of process and change. Certainly this book has presented much of the latter within its structural frame of reference. However, in the present conclusion, I can make only a few particularly pertinent generalizations about the immense field of social change. The most important controversies about macro-analysis that directly affect com-

[6] Failure to do this at *each* primary "stage" is a *major* shortcoming of Marxian theories of social evolution.

parative and evolutionary study have concerned the status of "factors." First, let me repeat, *any* processual outcome results from the operation of plural factors, all of which are mutually independent if there is scientific reason to distinguish among them. Here, the factors of production in economic analysis are logical prototypes.[7] In *this* sense, *no* claim that social change is "determined" by economic interests, ideas, personalities of particular individuals, geographical conditions, and so on, is acceptable. *All* such single-factor theories belong to the kindergarten stage of social science's development. *Any* factor is always interdependent with several others.

This elementary truth does not, however, preclude the hierarchical ordering of the factors. We have distinguished two basic, interrelated hierarchies—those of necessary conditions and of cybernetic control. At the most general level, the former runs from the physical, through the biological and psychological, to the social and cultural elements of action. The various sub-systems of these elements are similarly ordered. For example, within the social system, we have, following Eisenstadt, called attention to the negative effects of diminutions in mobile economic resources, both goods and manpower, upon the empires' maintenance of differentiated governmental structures. Such maintenance—as well as the prior development of such structures—evidently depends in the conditional sense on the availability of adequate mobile economic resources; if the latter "dry up" enough, "feudalization" occurs. However, the presence of such resources in a society does not automatically create the more differentiated type of government any more than atmospheric oxygen, though necessary for the emergence and maintenance of life, alone created human life.

The more important hierarchy for *our* purposes is the hierarchy of cybernetic control. I believe that basic innovation in the evolution of living systems, both organic and socio-cultural, does not occur automatically with increases of factors or resources at the lower (conditional) levels of the cybernetic hierarchies, but depends on analytically independent developments at their higher levels.[8] Essential as a large population may be for advanced social organization, the pressure of increasing numbers alone cannot create such organization—rather, it will release Malthusian checks. Properly developed, this argument also applies to economic productivity and political power.

In the sense, and *only* that sense, of emphasizing the importance of the cybernetically highest elements in patterning action systems, I am a cultural determinist, rather than a social determinist. Similarly, I believe that, within the social system, the normative elements are more important for social change than the "material interests" of constitutive units. The longer the time perspective, and the broader the system involved, the greater is the *relative* importance of higher, rather than lower, factors in the control hierarchy, regardless of whether it is pattern maintenance or pattern change that requires explanation.

Quite clearly, the present analysis has been couched on the level of the longest time-perspective and broadest comparative scope. Therefore, in *this* study, the emphasis in accounting for the main patterns and processes of change has been placed at the highest cybernetic level. This level is cultural rather

[7] Cf. Neil J. Smelser, *The Sociology of Economic Life* (Englewood Cliffs, New Jersey: Prentice-Hall, 1963).

[8] The reader may wish to refer back to Chap. 2 if he is unclear about these concepts.

than social and, within the cultural category, religious rather than secular. Within the social category, values and norms, especially legal norms, stand higher than political and economic interests. However, the consequence of following these priorities so exclusively involves determining the *broadest* patterns of change rather than explaining more detailed structures and processes.

Furthermore, it should be *very* clear that high-level innovations do *not* determine the subsequent development of the relevant systems so automatically that we may neglect all other factors. Quite the contrary; every developmental step depends on a long series of conditional factors. We formulate this dependence most generally in maintaining that higher-order factors (within the social system, normative factors) must successfully meet the conditions of becoming institutionalized in order to determine stable patterns of concrete action.[9] This means precisely that they must *gain control* over the relevant conditional factors. Most emphatically, this is *not* to say that the latter factors have only negligible importance. Rather, it merely claims, first, that to be controlled, conditional factors must be present in certain proper *combinations*, both in terms of one another and in terms of the normative factors, and, second, that conditional factors cannot create a new concrete order without *independent* innovation at a higher normative level.

Differences in non-cultural and non-normative conditions, and the ways in which they are combined with the cultural and normative factors, account for much of the variation that makes any linear theory of societal evolution untenable. Second, a major feature of the evolutionary process is that progressively greater differentiation increasingly frees the cybernetically higher factors from the narrow specifics of the lower-order conditioning factors, thus enabling the basic patterns of the cultural system to become more generalized, objectified, and stabilized.

These developments enhance the cultural system's potential to control wider ranges of varying factors at the conditional levels. Thus, a primitive society is not only limited in territory and population, but its culture is relatively specific to its conditions and does not readily integrate with those of other societies. An intermediate society is, in a sense, equivalent to the integration of a large number of primitive societies into one societal system. This presupposes, as we have strongly insisted, an integration at the cultural level, with special reference to the articulation obtaining between the cultural patterns and the normative system of the society.

A major theme in our discussion of the advanced intermediate empires, however, has been that such integrations of more particularistic, less generalized structural elements have typically been incomplete. In China, the local elements and the peasant cultures, above all, were only partially permeated by Confucian culture. In India, the integrative shortcomings involved both localism (sometimes tribalism) and the segmental, rather than differentiated aspects of caste diversity. In Rome and the Islamic empires, it was ethnic and local particularities which especially failed to be fully integrated into the political and legal structure of the empires, either as effectively "dominated" or, still more, as autonomously differentiated units.

The independence that components gain through differentiation, and its relation to variation, also has a time aspect. A differentiated component need

[9] Cf. Leon Mayhew, forthcoming book on law and social change.

not be bound to one concrete territory-and-population instance, nor to any particular period. Above all, culture, through documents and otherwise, can become relatively independent of particular "bearers" or members of a given society. Thus, a cultural system's consequences for subsequent societies cannot be inferred very directly from its mode of involvement in the societal structures of its origin, but must be analyzed in a much more complex framework.

We discussed the cases of Israel and Greece as particularly striking examples of this cultural-temporal independence. We would suggest that it presents a peculiarly difficult problem for the naive, Marxist-type sociological analysis to demonstrate how their enormous influence on later societies was really or in the last analysis based on the economic interests of either the originators or the adopters of these cultural patterns.

Great confusion over issues such as these has arisen from the dogma, often left implicit, that evolutionary theory must be "historical" in the sense of histori*cism*. Whether following Hegel, Marx, or later Germans such as Dilthey, historicism has characteristically denied the possibility or relevance of generalized *analytical* theory (which systematically treats the interdependence of independently variable factors) in explaining temporally sequential socio-cultural phenomena. Particularly in challenging this idea, Durkheim and Weber introduced a new era in sociological science. Once the problem of causal imputation is formulated analytically, the old chicken and egg problems about the priorities of ideal and material factors simply lose significance. I hope that the present treatment of the problems of societal evolution, though brief, will help lay to rest this ghost of our nineteenth-century intellectual past.

selected references

The recent phases of sociological concern with social evolution and the analytical comparison of societies stem largely from the classical studies of Max Weber, especially *The Theory of Social and Economic Organization* (Glencoe, Ill.: The Free Press, 1947); *The Sociology of Religion* (Boston: Beacon Press, 1963); and the other sections of *Wirtschaft und Gesellschaft*, a complete English translation of which will be published soon. As Robert Bellah has shown in his essay "Durkheim and History" (*American Sociological Review*, August 1959), Durkheim—for example, in *The Division of Labor in Society* (New York: Macmillan, 1933); and *Professional Ethics and Civic Morals* (London: Routledge and K. Paul, 1957)—developed very similar perspectives. *Theories of Society* (New York: The Free Press of Glencoe, 1961), edited by T. Parsons, E. Shills, K. Naegele, and J. Pitts, contains basic readings on social theory, along with introductory essays by Talcott Parsons and the other editors that interrelate analytical and evolutionary perspectives. "Religious Evolution" by Robert Bellah and "Evolutionary Universals in Society" by Talcott Parsons (both in the *American Sociological Review* for June 1964), present more recent developments in evolutionary theory. The fundamental distinction between general and special evolution is essayed in M. Sahlins and E. Service, *Evolution and Culture* (Ann Arbor: University of Michigan Press, 1960).

Durkheim's *The Elementary Forms of the Religious Life* (London: Allen & Unwin, 1915), remains the basic work concerned with primitive societies. *Structural Anthropology* (New York: Basic Books, 1963); and *Primitive Thought* (forthcoming) by Claude Levi-Strauss, present a theoretical position which is very influential in contemporary anthropology. The best introduction to modern kinship analysis is Rodney Needham's brief *Structure and Sentiment* (Chicago: University of Chicago Press, 1962). Lloyd Warner's *A Black Civilization* (New York: Harper Torchbooks, 1964) is an interesting general account of an Australian aboriginal society; W. E. H. Stanner's *On Aboriginal Religion* (Sydney: Oceania Monographs, 1963) is more recent and specialized. *African Political Systems* (London: Oxford University Press, 1940), edited by M. Fortes and E. E. Evans-Pritchard; *African Systems of Kinship and Marriage* (London: Oxford University Press, 1950), edited by A. R. Radcliffe-Brown and D. Forde, and *African Worlds* (London: Oxford University Press, 1954), edited by D. Forde, contain useful essays on various aspects of selected African tribes. R. Firth's *Primitive Polynesian Economy* (London: Routledge, 1939) is a good analysis of economic processes in a primitive society.

The Face of the Ancient Orient (Garden City: Anchor, 1962), by S. Moscati, is a clear introduction to the archaic societies of the ancient Near East. Henri Frankfort's *Kingship and the Gods* (Chicago: University of Chicago Press, 1948) is masterful in treating the relations between the political and religious aspects of archaic societies and in comparing the Egyptian and Mesopotamian civilizations. J. Wilson's *The Culture of Ancient Egypt* (Chicago: Phoenix Books, 1951) is more concerned with economic and community organization, as is H. W. F. Sagg's *The Greatness That Was Babylon* (New York: Hawthorn, 1962).

Max Weber's "The Social Psychology of the World Religions" and "Religious Rejections of the World and their Directions," in *From Max Weber* (New York: Galaxy Books, 1958), edited by H. H. Gerth and C. W. Mills; and S. N.

Eisenstadt's *The Political Systems of Empires* (New York: The Free Press of Glencoe, 1963) are outstanding as general comparative treatments of intermediate societies.

Weber's *The Religion of China* (Glencoe, Ill.: The Free Press, 1951) remains the best general sociological analysis of traditional China. J. K. Fairbank's *The United States and China* (Cambridge: Harvard University Press, 1959) contains a good brief outline of Chinese social history. Fung Yu-Lan's *A Short History of Chinese Philosophy* (New York: Macmillan, 1962) is a clear introduction to Chinese culture. Chang Chung-Li, *The Chinese Gentry* (Seattle: University of Washington Press, 1955); and Marion Levy, *The Family Revolution in Modern China* (Cambridge: Harvard University Press, 1949) are leading analyses of key aspects of Chinese society.

The Wonder That Was India (New York: Evergreen, 1959), by A. L. Basham and especially *Philosophies of India* (Cleveland: Meridian, 1956) by Heinrich Zimmer, are excellent general treatments of Indian civilization.

The work of H. A. R. Gibb comprises an excellent introduction to Islam, particularly his brief *Mohammedanism* (New York: Galaxy Books, 1962); and his study with H. Bowen, *Islamic Society and the West* (London: Oxford University Press, 1957). G. E. von Grunebaum's *Medieval Islam* (Chicago: Phoenix Books, 1961) is also reliable and interesting.

A good introduction to Roman history is *Rome* (New York: Galaxy Books, 1960) by M. Rostovtzeff. R. Syme's *The Roman Revolution* (London: Clarendon Press, 1939) is a detailed analysis of the processes by which the Empire emerged at the end of the Republic. *The Legacy of Rome* (Oxford: Clarendon Press, 1923), edited by C. Bailey, contains several fine essays on specific aspects of Roman society.

Though somewhat dated, Weber's *Ancient Judaism* (Glencoe, Ill.: The Free Press, 1952) remains unmatched for breadth and sociological insight among treatments of early Israel. Martin Buber's *Moses* (New York: Harper Torchbooks, 1958); and *The Prophetic Faith* (New York: Harper Torchbooks, 1960) are extraordinarily fine studies of the religious tradition; W. F. Albright's *From Stone Age to Christianity* (Garden City: Anchor Books, 1957) adds archaeological to documentary evidence in tracing the development of Hebrew society. Werner Jaeger's *Paideia*, Vol. 1 (New York: Oxford University Press, 1945) is probably the foremost modern discussion of Greek culture. *A History of Greek Religion* (New York: Norton, 1964), by M. P. Nilsson, is a sound treatment of its complicated subject. V. Ehrenberg presents a well-balanced survey of Greek political organization in *The Greek State* (New York: Norton, 1964).

index

Aboriginal Australia, 35-41
economy, 36, 38
marriage, 36, 38
religion, 38-40
social structure, 36-38
technology, 40
warfare, 40
Abraham, 83, 97
Ackerman, Charles D., 44*n*
Action system, 5-9, 29-35
subsystems, 29
table, 28
Adaptation, 22, 28, 29
Adaptive upgrading, 22
Advanced intermediate societies, 69-94
China, 71-77
India, 77-82
Islamic Empire, 82-86
Roman Empire, 86-93
Advanced primitive societies, 42-50
economy, 42-43
marriage, 42, 46
political system, 50
religion, 45, 49
types, 47-50
warfare, 49
African kingdoms, 47
Albright, W. F., 97*n*, 99*n*
Alexander, 107
Allah, 83, 86
Allocation, 16
Animal symbolism, 39
Archaic societies, 51-68
Ancient Egypt, 52-62
Mesopotamian Empire, 62-68
political system, 52
religion, 52
Arensberg, Conrad, 67*n*
Aristotle, 106-107
Arunta tribe, 37
Aryans, 78, 79
Ashoka, 81

Baal cults, 99
Babylonia, 101
Bailey, Cyril, 87*n*, 90*n*, 93*n*
Bales, Robert F., 12*n*
Barker, Sir Ernest, 87*n*, 93
Basham, A. L., 81*n*
Behavioral organism, 5, 6, 8-9, 28, 29
as environment to society, 15-16
Bellah, Robert N., 24, 26*n*, 39, 51, 55, 71, 86*n*
Bemba tribe, 50, 52
Beyer, W. C., 105*n*
Brahmans, 78, 79
Braidwood, Robert J., 52*n*
Broom, Leonard, 19*n*
Brown, Roger, 6*n*
Buber, Martin, 97, 99*n*, 100*n*, 101*n*
Buddhism, 78, 80, 81, 95
Bultmann, Rudolph, 99*n*, 100*n*, 102*n*
Burke, Kenneth, 61*n*, 106*n*

Caste system, 1, 4
Chang, Chung-Li, 75*n*
Change, 21
process and, 20-21
Ch'in dynasty, 71
China, 1, 4, 62, 69, 71-77, 95
economy, 75-76, 77
education, 72
legal system, 77
religion, 71-72
social structure, 73-75
Chomsky, Noam, 20*n*, 35*n*
"Chosen people," 83, 97, 98
Chou society, 71-72
Cochrane, Charles N., 92*n*
Code Napoleon, 65
Code of Hammurabi, 65-66
Collectivities, 18-19
Confucianism, 71-73, 77, 78, 80
Confucius, 72, 77
Constitutive symbolism, 33-35, 51, 64, 70, 100
Cottrell, Leonard S., Jr., 19*n*
Coulborn, R., 54*n*
Covenant, 83, 97, 98, 100-101
Craft literacy, 52
Creel, H. G., 71*n*, 75, 76, 77*n*
Cult systems, 52, 54-55, 76, 98-99
Cultural system, 5, 6, 8-9, 28, 29
as environment to society, 11
Cumont, Franz, 93*n*
Cybernetic control, 9, 17, 21, 113
Cybernetic hierarchy, 11-14

Daniel, 99, 100
Darwin, Charles, 30, 111
David, 97
de Bary, W. T., 79*n*, 81*n*
de Zulueta, F., 87*n*, 88*n*
Decision, 20-21
Delphi, 103
Deutsch, Karl W., 9*n*
Developmental breakthrough, 23
Differentiation, 22-25, 33, 43
Dilthey, Wilhelm, 115
Dodds, E. R., 106*n*
"Dravidian" peoples, 78
Dreckmeier, Charles, 78*n*
Durkheim, Emile, 33*n*, 35, 38, 40, 51, 115

Easton, David, 13*n*
Eckstein, Harry, 10*n*
Economy, 17, 25, 28, 29
aboriginal Australia, 36, 38
advanced primitive societies, 42-43
China, 75-76
Egypt, 56
Mesopotamian Empire, 63, 67
Edgerton, William F., 53*n*, 54*n*, 55*n*, 56*n*, 57*n*, 58*n*
Education, 72
Ego, 15
Egypt:
ancient, 52-62, 95
economy, 56
legal system, 58-59
literacy, 53
political system, 54, 55-56, 57
religion, 59-61
technology, 56
Ehrenberg, Victor, 103*n*, 104*n*, 105*n*
Eisenstadt, S. N., 57*n*, 62, 70*n*, 77*n*, 85*n*, 91*n*, 110*n*, 113
Emerson, Alfred, 6*n*, 30*n*
Enforcement, 10, 14
Epidaurus, 104
Erotic complex, 31-32
Evans-Pritchard, E. E., 43*n*, 47*n*, 48*n*, 49, 50, 61*n*
Evolution, 2, 3, 20-21, 21-24, 109-111
and variability, 2, 3, 112
evolutionary change, 21-24
organic, 30, 109-111
societal, 20-21
socio-cultural, 2, 109-115
stages, 26-27

Fairbank, John King, 71*n*, 76*n*
Fashoda, 48
Fei, Hsiao-Tung, 76*n*
Firth, Raymond, 43*n*
Forde, Daryll, 46*n*, 48*n*, 50*n*
Fortes, Meyer, 43*n*, 47*n*, 49, 50
Fowler, W. Warde, 87*n*, 104*n*
Frankfort, A., 53*n*
Frankfort, H. A., 65*n*
Frankfort, Henri, 53*n*, 54*n*, 57*n*, 59*n*, 60, 61, 63*n*, 65, 98

Freud, Sigmund, 12, 15, 31, 60
Fullani, 51
Fundamentalism, 23

Geertz, Clifford, 84*n*
Gerard, Ralph W., 31*n*
Ghazzali, Al, 85
Gibb, H. A. R., 83*n*, 85
Gibbon, Edward, 93
Gluckman, Max, 49*n*
Goody, Jack, 26*n*, 42*n*
Gordon, Cyrus H., 96*n*, 103*n*
Granet, Marcel, 73
Greece, 21, 25, 53, 69, 103-108
  culture, 103, 107
  religion, 104, 105-106
  social structure, 103, 104-105, 107
Grinker, Roy, 6*n*, 30*n*
Grunebaum, von, Gustave E., 84*n*, 86*n*

Halle, Morris, 20*n*
Hammurabi, code of, 65-66
Han dynasty, 71, 75
Hardin, Donald, 103*n*
Harlow, Harry F., 31*n*
Harnack, Adolf, 87*n*
Hathor, 59, 60, 61
Hay, S. N., 79*n*
Hegel, Georg W. F., 115
Hesiod, 103
Hignett, C., 105*n*
Hinduism, 78, 80-81
Hobbes, Thomas, 7
Homer, 103
Horus, 59, 60, 61
Hsien, 75
Hsu, Francis L. K., 76*n*
Hubert, Henri, 24*n*
Human action system, 5-9, 28-29

Id, 15
Incarnation, 79
Incest, 36, 39, 59-60, 106
India, 69, 77-82, 95
  caste system, 1, 4,
  language, 78
  religion, 78, 79-80, 81
  social structure, 78-79, 80-81
"Instinct" theories, 32
Integration, 22, 25, 28, 29
Interaction, 8, 20
Intermediate societies, 3, 51-94
  advanced intermediate, 69-94
  archaic, 51-68
Islamic empire, 4, 27, 69, 82-86
  legal system, 84-85
  political system, 84
  religion, 84, 85, 86
  social structure, 83
Israel, 21, 53, 96-102
  legal system, 99
  literacy, 101-102
  religion, 98
  social structure, 97

Jacobsen, Thorkild, 53*n*, 65*n*
Jacobson, Roman, 20*n*
Jaeger, Werner, 103*n*, 106*n*, 107*n*
Jahweh, 53, 83, 97, 100-101, 102
Jainism, 80
Japan, 3, 95
Jesus Christ, 83
Job, 106
Jones, H. Stuart, 90*n*
Judaism, 99, 100-101
Jus civilis, 88
Jus gentium, 88-90

Karma, 79
Kinship system, 12, 13, 33, 35, 36, 38, 46, 48, 55, 74
Klausner, S. Z., 13*n*
Koranic law, 86
Ksatriyas, 78

Language, 5, 6, 20, 34
  India and, 78
  oral, 31
  written, 26-27, 51
Latourette, Kenneth Scott, 71*n*
Law enforcement, 14, 16-17
Leach, Edmund, 37*n*, 39*n*, 42*n*, 44*n*
Learning, 6, 30
Legal system, 27
  China, 77
  Egypt, 58-59
  Islamic Empire, 84-85
  Israel, 99
  Mesopotamian Empire, 65-67
  Roman Empire, 87, 88, 89
Lessa, William, 41*n*
Levi-Strauss, Claude, 33*n*, 36*n*, 38*n*, 39*n*
Levite tribe, 102
Levy, Marion, 75*n*
Levy, Reuben, 83*n*, 85*n*
Li, 73-74
Lienhardt, Godfrey, 48*n*

Maat, 61
Magic, 40
Malinowski, Bronislaw, 40*n*
Marriage, 36-38, 42, 46
  aboriginal Australia, 36-38
  advanced primitive societies, 42, 46
Marsh, Robert M., 74*n*
Marx, Karl, 115
Mauss, Marcel, 24*n*, 33*n*, 35*n*
Mayhew, Leon, 114*n*
Mayr, Ernst, 6*n*, 31*n*
Mecca, 83
Medina, 83
Meek, Theophile James, 97*n*, 98*n*, 102*n*
Mendenhall, George E., 97, 98*n*
Mercier, P., 50*n*
Merton, Robert K., 19*n*
Mesopotamian Empire, 25, 52-53, 62-68, 95, 101
  economy, 63, 67
  legal system, 65-67
  literacy, 63
  political system, 63-65
  religion, 63-64, 68
  social structure, 62-63
Middleton, Russell, 59*n*
Modern societies, 3
  Japan, 3
  origin, 3
  Soviet Union, 3
  United States, 3
Mogul Empire, 82
Mohammed, 83, 84, 86
Moral causation, 79
Mosaic decalogue, 99
Moscati, Sabatino, 59*n*, 62*n*, 63*n*, 64*n*, 65*n*, 66*n*, 67*n*, 96*n*, 99*n*
Moses, 83, 97, 99
Murngin tribe, 34, 37, 39, 40
Muslims, 82, 84

Nadel, S. F., 45*n*, 47*n*, 50
Naegele, Kasper D., 7*n*, 111*n*
Nakamura, Hajime, 80*n*, 81*n*
Napoleon, Code, 65
Needham, Rodney, 35*n*, 36*n*, 41*n*, 42*n*
Nelson, Benjamin, 13*n*
Nilsson, Martin P., 89*n*, 91*n*, 103*n*, 104*n*
Nock, A. D., 89*n*, 93*n*, 107*n*
Normative order, 18, 28
"Norms," 18-19
Nupe society, 50, 51
Nyikang, 48

Occupational specialization, 43
Oedipus, 106
Olmstead, A. T., 64*n*, 65*n*, 103*n*
Olympia, 103-104
Osiris, 60, 61

Pan-religionism, 38
Pardue, Peter, 81*n*
Parsons, Talcott, 2*n*, 7*n*, 9*n*, 10*n*, 12*n*, 13*n*, 14*n*, 15*n*, 19*n*, 20*n*, 25*n*, 33*n*, 38*n*, 52*n*, 111*n*
Pattern-maintenance, 25, 28, 29

as environment to society, 11-15
Pearson, Harry, 67*n*
Personality system, 5, 7, 8-9, 28, 29
as environment to society, 11-15
Philip of Macedon, 107
Philosophic breakthrough, 70
Physical-organic environment, 9
Physical skills, 35
Ping-ti, Ho, 74*n*
Pitts, Jesse R., 7*n*, 111*n*
Plato, 106
Polanyi, Karl, 67*n*
Political systems:
advanced primitive societies, 50
Egypt, 54, 55-56, 57
Islamic Empire, 84
Mesopotamian Empire, 63-65
Roman Empire, 87, 89, 90-91
Shilluk society, 48
Polis structures, 49, 82, 87, 103-104
Polity, 25, 28, 29
Polygyny, 46, 55
Pound, Roscoe, 2
Prescriptive system, 41, 42
Primitive societies, 30-50
aboriginal Australia, 35-41
advanced, 42-50
components, 32-35
Problem of order in society, 7
"Problems of meaning," 8
Process and change, 20-21
Procreation theme, 61-62
Property complex, 46
Prophetic movement, 101
Puritanism, 77

Qur'an, 84, 85

Re, 59
Reincarnation, 79
Religion, 33, 38-40
aboriginal Australia, 38-40
advanced primitive societies, 45, 49
China, 71-72
Egypt, 59-61
Greece, 104, 105-106
India, 78, 79-80, 81
Islamic Empire, 84, 85, 86
Israel, 98
Mesopotamian Empire, 63-64, 68
Roman Empire, 88, 92-93
Shilluk society, 48
Resurrection theme, 61-62
Rheinstein, Max, 27*n*
Richards, Audrey, 50
Ritual, 39-40
Roles, 18-19
Roman Empire, 4, 25, 27, 69
legal system, 87, 88 , 89
political system, 87, 89, 90-91
religion, 88, 92-93
social structure, 86-87
Rosenthal, E. I. J., 86*n*

Saggs, H. W. F., 63*n*, 66*n*, 67*n*
Sangha, 81
Sanscrit, 78
Schapera, I., 43*n*, 47*n*, 50*n*
"Seed-bed" societies, 95-108
Greece, 103-108
Israel, 96-102
Self-sufficiency, 16-18
Shari'a, 84, 85
Shih, 71
Shilluk society, 47-50, 52
government, 48
religion, 48
Shils, Edward A., 7*n*, 111*n*
Simpson, George Gaylord, 6*n*
Skills, 31
Slavery, 66, 92
Smelser, Neil J., 15*n*, 16*n*, 113*n*
Social structure:
aboriginal Australia, 36-38
China, 73-75
Greece, 103, 104-105, 107
India, 78-79, 80-81
Islamic Empire, 83
Israel, 97
Mesopotamian Empire, 62-63
Roman Empire, 86-87
Social system, 5, 7, 8-9, 29
concept of, 8
environments, 9
Socialization, 12
Societal community, 10-18, 45
environments, 10-16, 28
self-sufficiency, 16-18
table, 29
Society:
concept, 1-2, 9-10, 17
defined, 2, 9
intermediate, 3, 51-94
modern, 3
primitive, 3, 30-50
"seed-bed," 95-108
structural components, 18-20
Socrates, 106
Solomon, 97, 98
Sophocles, 106
Soviet Union, 1, 3
Species-type, 6
Spencer, Herbert, 109-110
Spuhler, J. N., 31*n*
Stanner, W. E. H., 39, 41
Stratification, 47, 54, 58, 89
Sudra, 71, 78
Sufist movements, 85
Superego, 15
Symbolic communication, 33
Syme, Ronald, 89*n*, 90*n*, 91*n*

Talmudic law, 27, 85
Tao, 73
Tawney, R. H., 77*n*
Tax, Sol, 109*n*
Technology, 15-16, 17, 33
aboriginal Australia, 40
Egypt, 56
Totemism, 34, 38
Troeltsch, Ernest, 93*n*

"Ultimate reality," 8, 9, 29
Umma, 83, 85, 86, 93
United States, 1, 3
Untouchables, 78
Urbs, 87

Vaicyas, 78
Values, 18-19
Variation, 2, 3
Vedic tradition, 78-79
Voegelin, Eric, 67*n*, 100*n*, 101*n*, 103*n*, 104*n*, 106*n*
Vogt, Evon Z., 41*n*

Warfare:
aboriginal Australia, 40
advanced primitive societies, 49
Warner, W. Lloyd, 34*n*, 36*n*, 38*n*, 39*n*, 40, 41*n*
Watt, Ian, 26*n*
Wawilak sisters, 39
Weber, Max, 4, 8, 27, 50, 53, 56, 60, 72*n*, 75*n*, 76, 77, 78*n*, 79, 80, 81*n*, 82*n*, 92, 97, 98*n*, 99, 100*n*, 101*n*, 102*n*, 105*n*, 107*n*, 111, 115
Weiler, R., 79*n*
Welfare state, 56
Wiener, Norbert, 9*n*
Willey, Gordon, 52*n*
Wilson, John A., 53*n*, 54*n*, 55*n*, 56*n*, 57*n*, 58*n*, 59*n*, 61*n*, 65*n*
Wittfogel, K. A., 58*n*
Wollunqua, 34, 39
Wollunqua-Wawilak myth, 39

Yang-Yin dichotomy, 73
Yarrow, A., 79*n*
Yu, 34
Yu-lan, Fung, 72*n*, 73*n*
Yurlunggur, 34, 39*n*

Zimmer, Heinrich, 79*n*, 80*n*, 81*n*
Zulu kingdom, 49